I0769839

Challenges of a 21st Century Progressive

Norbert Bufka

Acknowledgment
I am very grateful to my wife Sue for proofreading and invaluable editing suggestions that make this book more readable. I am also grateful to Edward Hutchison for his proofreading and edits.

Publisher:
Norbert Bufka
norbert609@sbcglobal.net
Norbert Bufka's books are described and for sale on his updated website:
Website www.thisonly.org.

Printed in the United States.

Contents

Introduction   **1**

Worldview   *3*

1.   **Our Great Country**..

The Flag   *10*

American Exceptionalism   *12*

2. Government   **15**

We, the People   *15*
Native Americans   16
Enslaved People   17
Women   17

Compromise   *18*

Federal Government   *20*
President   21
Congress   21
Supreme Court   22

State and local governments   *24*
State courts   24
Local Governments   25

Is the Government Doing Its Job?   *25*

3. Freedom   **28**

Prayer in Public Schools   *30*

Religion and Politics   *31*

Muslims   *33*
Mosque in New York   34

Religious Freedom Restoration Act   *35*
Jesus Served All People   36
Possible Outcomes of this Law   37

Abortion and Contraceptives   *38*

Creationism and evolution   38

4. All Lives Have Dignity   **41**

The Unborn   43

Minorities   44

Gays   48
  Gay Marriage   51

Immigrants   53

Victims of Gun Violence   57
  Police Shootings   60
  Mass Shootings   61
  Solution   62

Prisoners   64
  Who Is in Prison?   65
  Why?   65
  Cost of Correctional System   66
  Crime Rates   67
  Prison Privatization   67
  Life in Prison   68
  Reform   68

The Elderly   69

All Lives Matter   69

5. Everything Is Interconnected   **70**

Economy   70
  Capitalism   70
  Technological Revolution   75
  Socialism   76
  Managing the Economy   78

Health care   80
  Drugs   83

Environment   84
  Global warming   87

Infrastructure   87

Education 88

6. Taxes Are the Dues To Be American **93**

Federal Income Tax 94

Social Security or Payroll Tax (FICA) 96

Tax Reform 97
Personal Income Tax Reform 99
Reform of Social Security 100
Reform of Business Taxes 101

7. Foreign Policy **104**

Security 105

The Middle East 105

War 106

Peacemaking 108

8. Voting with Integrity **111**

Restrictions on voting 112
Voter ID 113
Voter Registration 113
Early Voting 114
Restoring Voting Rights to Felons 114
Gerrymandering 114
The Electoral College 115

Reform of voting procedures 117

9. The General Welfare **119**

About the Author **124**

Bibliography **125**

Endnotes **132**

Introduction

In 1960 Sen Barry M. Goldwater published his book, *The Conscience of a Conservative*. I was a very right-wing Republican in those days and voraciously read his book. I underlined nearly everything and quoted from it often. By 1972 I had undergone a transformation and voted for George McGovern for President. I have not wavered from my progressive thinking since then.

In June 2017 Sen. Jeff Flake (R-AZ) wrote *Conscience of a Conservative: A Rejection of Destructive Politics and a Return to Principle* in order to bring back the principles and values of the modern conservative movement which Goldwater started. Flake wrote, "I believe in the power of conservative principles to transform lives, lift countries, alleviate suffering, and make people prosperous and free." I believe progressive values will better accomplish the same things. [1]

Flake declared that his party lost its princilples in the 2016 campaign and that the Democrats are not the enemy. I couldn't agree more. With those two thoughts in mind, I hope he and the Democrats can work together to solve our country's problems and move it forward. The Tax Cuts and Jobs Act was clearly not a conservative bill.

Conservatives are not the only ones with values and principles upon which our country was founded. I too believe in "life, liberty, and the pursuit of happiness" for all Americans and all who wish to be Americans, but I believe in equality of all citizens and the right to vote. I too believe in limiting government but there are some aspects of American life which naturally belong in the public domain and are the purview of government.

Where we progressives differ from conservatives is in the application of those principles and values which we all hold dear. Sometimes they come in conflict with each other and it is challenging to come up with suitable compromises that benefit the most people.

Every aspect of public policy is interrelated. Nothing stands alone nor should it be dealt with alone. One of my biggest complaints about conservative think tanks is that they offer comments or solutions based on a free market alone.

Finally, the biggest difference between conservative and progressives is that our focus is on people and conservatives would rather focus on principles. This may seem harsh and conservatives may object, but it has been pretty clear to me that conservatives would rather let people die than break their understanding of a principle. A case in point is the attempted repeal of the Affordable Care Act with a plan that would remove millions of people from insurance and therefore access to adequate health care. Conservatives did even worse in the Tax Cut Act by repealing the individual mandate in the Affordable Care Act. This will not only end insurance coverage for millions, it will be the end of hospitals in rural areas of our country because they will lack the revenue to stay functional, leading to more millions without adequate access to health care. Repealing the nandate will also push premiums up. Health care is one of those rights that must not be a mere product of a capitalistic venture. Conservatives tell us progressives whenever we say more money is needed for a problem, that money is not the solution. Yet **their** bottom line is always money.

The Declaration of Independence says in part, "We hold these truths to be self-evident, that all men are created equal, that they are endowed by their Creator with certain unalienable Rights, that among these are Life, Liberty and the pursuit of Happiness."

Mark Levin, in his book *Rediscovering Americanism: And the Tyranny of Progressivism,* quotes this document as a starting point for his tirade against progressivism. He quotes numerous philosophers and founders of our country to show how the progressive movement has denied these values and eroded American ideals. He also quoted from the Virginia Declaration of Rights, which was adopted less than a month before the Declaration of Independence. This document also upholds the rights of life and liberty and adds the right to own property, which I am sure is why Levin quoted this document. Levin claims property rights are as sacred as life and liberty. Levin makes the claim that we progressives reject these fundamental values because we do not believe them to be absolute. He is right. These rights are not absolute, especially property rights. Even the right to life is not absolute although it is a higher value than property.

Progressives also believe in the truth that all people are created equal, which is in the same sentence as "life, liberty, and the pursuit of happiness" in the Declaration of Independence. We also believe in the rest of the Preamble to the Constitution which calls for a more perfect union, justice, domestic tranquility, the common defense, and the general welfare of all citizens. These too are high values of our founding fathers and our country. While the founders intended these values to be fulfilled in the articles of the Constitution, they also opened the door to creative ways to make these values become real and not just words on a parchment. Making these words become reality is precisely why the Constitution has been amended twenty-seven times.

The pursuit of happiness is generally accepted to mean that a person can do whatever he or she wants. It is tied closely to liberty. The pre-eminent American historian, David McCulloch, said that for the founding fathers, "Happiness is enlargement of one's being through the life of the mind and of the spirit." In other words, education was the door to greater happiness. George Washington regretted all his life that he had not had a formal education. [2] Progressives strongly believe in the founding fathers' emphasis on the importance of universal public education as a means to happiness.

It is important to know the challenges facing our country, state, and local community. Then comes probably the most difficult task of all, finding out what the candidates think about these challenges. And that task is fraught with all kinds of difficulties because candidates want to appeal to the widest number of voters and so either are unclear about an issue or deliberately confuse the voter.

Of course, no one candidate will express views in complete harmony with your views so the final step is to grapple with the issues and set priorities on those issues before choosing a candidate. It is dangerous, however, to vote on one issue without considering the overall effect of a candidate's views on the common good.

Worldview

A value not often talked about is integrity. It essentially means acting according to one's most sacred beliefs and values. This integrity is not only a necessary quality of a candidate but also that of a responsible voter.

Integrity requires sincere and honest deliberation about what is best for our country. And this determination mostly depends on deep values. Integrity largely has to do with purifying our intentions and being honest about our motives. It is hard work and is essential in dealing with crises." [3]

One place to begin is to examine our world view. Everyone has a worldview. It involves the purpose and meaning of life. It encompasses the answer to the question: why am I here? It's a question that has been asked from the time human beings gained consciousness.

Each person's world view is formed by the many human experiences each one has: family upbringing, education, religion, our culture, jobs and just plain living. For many of us, I suspect, our world view is formed unconsciously or automatically. We don't generally examine all those aspects of our lives. Or if we do, the examination is cursory and sporadic rather than intentional.

My life experiences, for example, included birth into a Catholic family of boys on a farm in northern Michigan. I went to a local public school through the ninth grade. Then I went to a Catholic all boys boarding school for six years. Finally, I finished my bachelor's degree at a Catholic college in Grand Rapdis Michigan and a master's degree at a public university in central Illinois, followed by a Master of Pastoral Studies from a Catholic university many years later.

My work experiences involved farm labor, teaching, sales, and church ministry. My personal life of being a son, brother, husband and father too has influence me greatly.

Anyone could have those experiences, but it is how I assimilated them into my life that has led to my world view, which is reflected in all my writing and in all I say and do.

As A result of all these influences on our lives, our worldview may need revision. To examine our worldview, we need to

1) develop an open attitude,

2) communicate with others, especially those with different points of view,

3) be aware that learning is both formal and informal.

The most difficult area to amend in our world view, I think, is the one related to religion. Religion has a power that sometimes closes our minds to an openness to other points of view. Not all points of view are of equal importance nor are all values, even if we hold them dearly.

One aspect of our worldview is what we think about abundance and scarcity. I include these thoughts here because they are seldom mentioned in a discussion of worldview. A mentality of abundance starts with self-acceptance and acceptance of others. It means, in the words of a famous book, "I'm ok, you're ok". Among us are everything that you need to live, survive, and thrive. A hallmark quality of abundance thinking is love.

Love leads to sharing. Since you have abundance, you want to share what you have with others, sharing not only your material things, but your person and your very being.

In sharing with others, a spirit of cooperation develops. Through cooperation, much can be accomplished. For example, the rebuilding of lives and neighborhoods after a crisis, like hurricanes Harvey and Irma in 2017, are the fruits of cooperation.

On the other hand, there is the scarcity mentality. This view stems from the lack of belief in oneself and in each other. It assumes that because you are lacking, all are lacking and you must get what belongs to you before someone else gets it.

The primary emotion connected with scarcity is not hate, but rather fear – a trembling inside of the lack of worth. With a scarcity mentality, fear is the dominant motive for acting and not acting in any given situation. It keeps you from moving forward in your vocation or way of life. It keeps you from stretching your limits to really do what you want to do or could do.

Scarcity mentality breeds a spirit of selfishness: look out for yourself because what is available is limited. It's getting what you want and not caring about what others want or need.

Finally, scarcity mentality leads to conflict. If you are constantly seeking what you want, that will inevitably lead to a conflict with what someone else wants or has. Conflict resolution becomes necessary.

Scarcity mentality also leads to competition, a key element of capitalism. Competition generates new products and lower prices. Those are good things. Competition almost always means someone has to lose.

Advertising is another key element in capitalism. It makes us aware of products and services that are available. That's good. It can also be used to exploit people's scarcity mentality by insisting that you need what they are selling.

Chris Mercer on the Mercer Value website,[4] talked of this mentality in business. Scarcity depends on the individual performance, but abundance thinking depends on and benefits everyone from the designer to marketing to sales to secretary to consumer. [1] Abundance thinking is good for business.

Fear has been shamefully promoted by our leaders, especially after 9/11/01. It played a big part in the presidential campaign of 2016, leading to the election of Donald Trump. As a result, fear clutches the hearts of so many people that it is nearly impossible to arrive at reasonable solutions or courses of action. It would be well for us to remember the words of President Franklin Roosevelt, "The only thing we have to fear is fear itself."

This abundance/scarcity thinking points us in the direction of two different worldviews, which are quite opposite of each other. Many people are one or the other, but most people operate from a combination of these two ways of thinking, depending on the circumstances. So, the first question you might ask yourself in reviewing your worldview is this: Do I view the world as one of abundance or one of scarcity?

George P. Lakoff, an American cognitive linguist and philosopher, uses different language to describe the two opposing worldviews. He says one is a nurturing parent and the other is strict father. A nurturing parent worldview has three main traits, he says, "empathy, responsibility for yourself and others, and a commitment to do your best not just for yourself, but for your family, your community, your country, and the world." [5] These traits are intimately connected with the fundamental American values of equality, life, liberty, and the pursuit of happiness.

Life must be protected from disease and unwanted attacks. Workers and the environment must be protected from exploitation. The pursuit of happiness is reached when one is fulfilled and this cannot be done alone. All prosperity comes from the freedom to be involved with others in the family, community, work, or government. Lakoff said, ""Trust, honesty, and open communication are fundamental progressive values." [6] All progressive values flow from a nurturant worldview.

A strict father worldview, Lakoff says, believes that "the world is a dangerous place." This view believes that children are born bad and must be taught to be good through physical punishment. In this way they will learn to be morally good and will prosper. Those who aren't prosperous are clearly not morally good, this worldview says. Obedience is a key quality. The morality being taught is self-interest. If all seek their self-interest, then all

---

[1] For more information about these two ways of thinking, check out http://www.geocities.com/Heartland/2964/15thSunday-a.html for a sermon based on the parable of the sower and God's lavish abundance and http://www.healinghealthcareassoc.org/documents/abundance-vs-scarcity.pdf for more information on the characteristics.

will prosper and there is no need for social programs. In fact, social programs are immoral, according to this strict father worldview. Tax cuts reward the good people, this worldview says, and it punishes those who are not prospering by cutting off social programs.

These two worldviews extend to foreign policy as well. The nurturant parent sees the world as a family of nations. Some need help. The strict father sees the same family, but the U. S. is the father and it tells the others what to do.

An aspect of our American culture is a very deep racism that permeates nearly all our discourse both in public and private. It is not confined to one worldview but is more apt to be found in the strict father worldview because the strict father does not believe in equality. An extension of this world view places the male ahead of women and the white male over all people of color.

After the Civil Rights Act of 1965, people were generaly inclined to make themselves aware of racist ideas and this drove the racist mentality to the fringes of society. In the last thirty years, however, and especially since the presidential election of 2016, racist elements have become mainstream. They are openly expressed by the advisors to our President and other national leaders. The white nationalist rally at Charlottesville, NC on August 13, 2017 is an example of such open movement, with white nationalists, Neo-Nazis, and Ku Klux Klan members in attendance. President Trump did not condemn the supremacists for the violence that occurred, but said they were "very fine people." [7].

Ibram X. Kendi, one of the nation's leading scholars of racism and founder of a new antiracism center at American University, wrote that a racist idea "is any concept that regards one racial group as inferior or superior to another racial group in any way." [8] Racist ideas permeate all issues we face as a nation.

With all these thoughts in mind I urge you to read this book with as much openness as possible, let yourself be challenged by the ideas presented here, and use them to affect to your worldview and prepare to engage in our national conversation. These actions will prepare you to vote responsibly.

1. Our Great Country

Our country was founded on principles of equality and justice. These were part of the moral fabric of the founders who wrote our initial documents of the Declaration of Independence and later the Constitution. When the delegates met to write the Constitution, they were thinking about how to make better the failed Articles of Confederation.

While the Declaration of Independence and the Constitution represent a spirit that we honor with a sacredness and reverence akin to religious fervor and God-like adoration, we must remember that these founders were human beings operating out of their culture, education and experience. The Constitution, for example, was written in secret sessions. Then the authors of the Constitution asked states to hold ratifying conventions before they had a chance to read it. The document was soon made available for reading and there was so much opposition that Alexander Hamilton, James Madison, the father of the Constitution, and John Jay, wrote essays in defense of this new Constitution. [2]

Many people objected to this new Constitution because it had no Bill of Rights and so the Congress proposed twelve amendments to this Constitution. Ten of them were approved and have become known as our Bill of Rights. As a result, the Constitution was finally approved by nine states and went into effect in 1788. The Bill of Rights and all the amendments are a part of the Constitution, a fact which many people, including politicians, seem to forget.

The founders of our country did not have a magic wand nor were they the human hand of God. Most of them were Deists although many had membership in a Christian Church. They were all white male human beings, who fashioned these documents to the best of their ability and then made changes almost immediately. The Constitution has been amended seventeen more times since 1791 to reflect changes in our country and our culture.

The process of civil debate, which the founders used, is one of the ways we are great. But even there we failed miserably when debate turned to war among our own citizens. That war (1861-1865) was a valuable lesson that needs to be reviewed in these times of violent rhetoric and ideological polarization so we don't make that same mistake again.

Equality is another highly regarded American value but it requires the work of human beings to achieve that in the real world. In the late 18th century equality meant the equality of white wealthy men, usually landowners, but not women, or the enslaved, or native Americans. We have made significant progress in some of these areas, but not in others. The nuts and bolts of politics is what brings about this equality for each generation. Today women are still seeking full equality not only in our civil affairs but in religions as well. Gays find themselves in a particularly unequal situation in public life today although great advancement was made with the Supreme Court decision that banning gay marriage was unconstitutional. Immigrants and children of immigrants too lack equality. Some politicians even want to take away citizenship from these children of immigrants, even though their citizenship is guaranteed by the 14th Amendment. The enslaved were set free in 1865 but their descendants still face huge hurdles in seeking equality because racist ideas still pervade our culture. Many still struggle with including all people of color in our society.

---

[2] These essays were published individually at first under the pseudonymn of Publius but were soon bound in book form and called the Federalist Papers.

This struggle for equality is also found in the work place where laborers have had to sacrifice their lives to form unions to secure safe working conditions, higher wages and more benefits from business owners. Much progress was made in this area in the late 19th and early 20th centuries despite the many attempts to bar these advances by our judicial system. Labor laws were declared unconstitutional for many years before finally being approved.

For the last thirty years the pendulum has again swung toward the big business owners and the very wealthy. The fundamental value of equality, much ignored and denied by conservatives, eludes the vast majority of people in the middle class and below while the top five percent wallow in luxuries at the expense of the lower and middle class workers. The income gap between the top paid and lowest paid has been growing so rapidly that the top 1% have wealth

unseen in this country for nearly a hundred years. Every effort to change this growing gap is criticized as "job killing" policies. A tax "reform" proposed in October 2017 included reducing the amount a person could contribute to a 401*k) plan in order to raise more taxes so that tax cuts could again be given to the millionaires and billionaires, a plan that has been carried out many times since President Reagan introduced the trickle-down theory of economics in 1982.

We were great in our work ethic and high standards of education and led the world in innovative technology as a result. Now we are dumbing down America while the rest of the world ratchets up its education and way of life. For example, a report in 2011 showed that Michigan Educational Assessment Program (MEAP) scores were inflated. The state told parents of fourth graders that 84% of their children were proficient in reading, but only 30% of these same students were proficient on the national test. Other scores in math and science were similarly disastrous.[9]

We need to make some hard decisions about the role of government in keeping with our values. We can't rely on jingoism to solve these problems. The solutions involve more than tax cuts for the wealthy and spending cuts by the government. Our infrastructure, education, and our very way of life in a world that is rapidly shrinking and changing are at stake.

The Flag

One of the ways we profess our greatness is reciting the Pledge of Allegiance to the flag. "I pledge allegiance to the flag of the United States of America and to the Republic for which it stands, one nation, indivisible, with liberty and justice for all."

Along with millions of others, I grew up reciting this Pledge in grade school. It was an honor to do so. Even though we call this a pledge to the flag, it is really more of a pledge to the country of which we are citizens. Our flag is a powerful symbol that conjures up all kinds of feelings, depending on the circumstances in which the flag is displayed. In 1954 the phrase "under God" was added to the Pledge. In recent years that phrase has created some controversy.

In a civic parade on Memorial Day or any other national holiday, the flag generates feelings of civic pride, patriotism and good feelings about our country.

At a funeral when the flag is draped across a coffin, it evokes feelings of respect for the person who died and gratitude for service to the country.

In the raising of the flag at school or in front of the court house, it may evoke feelings of civic pride and joy in being a citizen of this country in this given locality.

Even a picture of the flag, such as this one at the Marine Corps Memorial at Arlington National Cemetery conjures up feelings of pride and accomplishment.

On the other hand, when the flag is waved in your face, figuratively or literally, to silence citizens who dissent from the prevailing policies of the government, it is a shameful disgrace of the flag. When used in this way, it promotes improper nationalism, "my country right or wrong".

When the flag is used to elicit loyalty to either a person or the ideology professed "in the name of America", it is shameful and evokes resentment and bad feelings about our country.

When it is used to show the power of the United States in the world, it evokes feelings of fear and anger rather than compassion and collaboration.

When it is used for such banal purposes as making clothes out of it, painting your mail box as if it were a flag, or using it to hawk sales during Presidents' Day, the flag loses its glory.

When the flag is burned in protest or is spit upon, or when one kneels rather than stands during the Pledge, these actions can evoke anger toward the protestors rather than sympathy for their cause.

When the flag is used to promote something it clearly does not symbolize, such as God or a religion, it can evoke animosity towards religion and religious groups.

In 2006 a so-called "flag burning" amendment was introduced in the House of Representatives for ratification by the states but it was defeated in the United States Senate by one vote. (Who says one vote doesn't mean anything?) This amendment says nothing about burning the flag, but rather "that Congress may pass laws that prohibit the desecration of the flag". In other words, it is a wide-open door to criminalize any activity associated with the flag. Could this proposed amendment be opening a Pandora's box?

We have all heard arguments that this amendment shouldn't be passed because it violates one of the fundamental freedoms we cherish: the freedom of speech and protest. If we look at other countries' laws, we maight gain some wisdom. Three of the countries that have anti-flag desecration laws are China, Iran, and Cuba. Are these the countries we wish to emulate in promoting freedom here at home?

In October 2017, Politico-Morning Consult poll showed that 72% of the Republicans and 46% of the Democrats polled favored making illegal the desecration or burning of the flag. The poll also revealed that "53 percent of Republicans and 49 percent of Latinos favor 'stripping a person of their U.S. citizenship if they burn the American flag.'"[10]

Indeed, the flag is a powerful symbol, but let's remember that it is only a symbol. What we are really pledging support to is the country – a nation of freedom loving people who recognize that we all lose freedom if individual liberties are taken away, especially freedom of speech.

American Exceptionalism

Basically, this phrase is used by some to mean that we have a unique American way of life, based on a strong belief in freedom, the practice of constitutional government, and free enterprise capitalism. [11] This meaning is appealing and has drawn millions of people to this country to pursue their dreams.

A strong promoter of American exceptionalism was the Republican candidate for Vice President in 2008, Sarah Palin. In her book, *America by Heart* [12] she ascribes to the above meaning and adds, "We're not saying we're better than anyone else, or that we have the right to tell people in other countries how to live their lives." These are fine words on paper, but it is easy to jump to a meaning of superiority. Palin does exactly that in her unquestioned support of the military everywhere in the world as a "defender of our freedoms". She also says the United States is "to be a shining city on a hill, a beacon of liberty and hope for all the peoples of the earth", a sentiment taken from the Old Testament as an inspiration for the Hebrew people. This image was used by President Reagan in his farewell address in 1988. This phrase, American exceptionalism, was used in various times in our history to show superiority and special privileges endowed by God.

American exceptionalism however ignores three vital aspects of American history. As recently as one hundred years ago our economic system was based on farming. Anyone could stake out a claim to some land and make a living. That's precisely what many of our immigrant ancestors did, including my grandfather. In other words, the dream of freedom and economic security was readily available to millions of people. That is no longer true. Our economy is largely urban and land is no longer easily acquired for farming.

This view also ignores the dependence of our greatness on the genocide of the Native Americans and the theft of their lands. It also ignores the enslavement of millions of Africans. The legacy of these two horrible aspects of our history is still being felt.

Palin and many others define constitutionalism as limited government. Then she praised the Kennedy space program as an example of American ingenuity and determination to achieve our goals. Does she not realize that this was a government program, totally contrary to her views on limited government and free market capitalism?

She also wrote that the civil rights laws of 1964-1965 "are great human achievements." Does she not realize that these acts are totally contrary to her philosophy of limited government? People in the 1960's who held her view staunchly opposed these acts.

To her credit Palin mentions family life and religion as key elements in our American way of life. She also emphasizes strongly that constitutionalism and capitalism both require high public morality for them to succeed. Adam Smith, the icon of capitalism, based his entire theory of the *Wealth of Nations* on this premise of morality. She also quoted John Adams to support her assertion of the need for public morality.

Palin uses every opportunity in her book to slam President Obama as one who does not believe in American exceptionalism and is therefore unfit to be our President. Richard Lowry and Ramesh Ponnuru in an article in *National Review* [13] criticized President Obama. But the exceptionalists have it wrong on all these counts.

Public morality has fallen to a new low. I am finally coming to the conclusion that our politicians on both sides of the aisle are not interested in the welfare of the US and its citizens but in their own wealth and reelection and power. They are in the pockets of big business leaders who are interested in their own personal wealth creation, not the benefits of the company they lead, much less their employees or the country. Some churches too have fallen into believeing in their own preservation rather than the values they profess and promote, leading to a crisis of faith and religious confusion. Bringing problems to light does not mean that I, as a progressive, believe that America is essentially flawed, as Palin wrote about progressives, but rather that these flawed traits and policies must be dealt with openly, honestly and constructively. From examining these flaws we can grow and gain new strength. Appealing to an emotional cry of American exceptionalism does not heal the polarization that exists today and obstructs progress. Unfortunately it has grown much worse since 2008.

Palin is right in saying that family life is at the heart of the raising of these values to a new consciousness, Just saying what she doesm howeverm will not make the problems of public morality and family life, not to mention national debt, the economy, and other crises, go away. Solving these problems will require efforts by all segments of our culture and way of life, including government, non-profits, business, education, and every citizen. The change truly requires a "fundamental transformation", not an appeal to jingoism

Our country is a great country and we can be proud of it. We can show our pride in many ways but there is no better way than by being aware of challenges to our deepest values and finding solutions to those challenges. These challenges will continue because people change and society changes as well as the culture of our society. New discoveries about human life and our world dictate that we must make changes from time to time.

2. Government

"We the People of the United States, in Order to form a more perfect Union, establish Justice, insure domestic Tranquility, provide for the common defence, promote the general Welfare, and secure the Blessings of Liberty to ourselves and our Posterity, do ordain and establish this Constitution for the United States of America."

When you read or hear these words of the Preamble to the Constitution I am sure your heart fills with patriotism and you stand taller. I know I do. There is something time-honored and personal knowing that I am part of the "We" that established the Constitution that still is the heart and soul of our representative democracy - a unique and experimental endeavor at self-government.

We, the People

As lofty as those sentiments are however, we would do ourselves a favor if we took a more careful look at the "We" of that document. 55 wealthy male landowners signed the Constitution. They wrote it in visionary language but also clearly for the benefit of the wealthy class they represented. And so the Constitution has continued to this day with 27

Amendments which limit the power of the few or extend freedom to more people. There were three major groups excluded from that collective "We".

Native Americans

Not only were the native inhabitants of this great land not included in that phrase, they were systematically moved from their lands by agreements, treaties, and bloody wars. These treaties were broken when it was to the advantage of the United States. Even after the Native Americans were put on their own reservations, they were not safe. When oil was discovered in the Oklahoma Indian Territory, suddenly the white settlers clamored for statehood and won it.

Today we raise our eyebrows in disdain at the genocide occurring around the world, but we fail to teach to our children the genocide our own government committed over several centuries until there was only a remnant left of the Native Americans in various locations, many times not near their original homelands.

Hatred of Native Americans began early with the saying in 1636 "the only good Indian was a dead Indian". After the bbloody Civil War, Gen. Philip Sheridan echoed the same sentiment, "The only good Indians I know are dead".[14] President U. S. Grant, however, appointed his friend Ely S. Parker to be head of the Bureau of Indian Affairs. Parker was of the Seneca tribe and the first non-white appointed to such a high office. Grant

16

was very progressive in working with the Native Americans. He wanted to develop a path to citizenship, but his plans were derailed by people like Sheridan and Gen. Sherman.

After many years on reservations and with little or no voice in their affairs or future, the United States government began to recognize fishing rights of the Native Americans and allowed them to fish freely. They were also given exclusive rights to own and operate casinos in some areas with profits distributed to all qualified members. Yet they continue to struggle for equality and inclusion.

Enslaved People

The first enslaved people were Africans brought to the colonies in 1619. There followed a very tragic but thriving slave trade until slavery was forbidden after our Civil War. Not only were these enslaved people excluded from being part of the "We", they were doubly insulted by being declared property and had no human rights in the Dred Scott decision. Adding more insult, they were counted as 3/5ths of a person for Congressional representation by white men, but they had no vote. This part of American history is taught but without, I suspect, the shame it should engender. Gouverneur Morris, the "brilliant" [15] author of the Preamble, was ardently opposed to slavery but was unable to convince a majority of the delegates.

Enslaved people were freed and guaranteed other rights by the 13th, 14th and 15th Amendments but were quickly segregated by law and other practices from being part of the "We, the people" through segregationist laws and practices, called "Jim Crow". These practices were allowed to happen because of racist ideas held by Americans all over the country, not just in the former Confederacy. Even now many of the descendants are separated from mainstream American life. The election of Barack Obama as President, though he is not a descendant of an enslaved person, represents an historic development in making "We the people" more inclusive.

In a surprising step backward for our country, Donald Trump was elected President in 2016.He is the antithesis of progress toward a more inclusive nation with his nativist, racist, and xenophobic ideas and policies.

Women

The largest class of people who were not part of the "We" were women. The colonial society was still very much a patriarchal society with remnants of the former practice of considering a woman as her husband's property. For example, in the 1790's Rachel Donelson, the future wife of Andrew Jackson, was not allowed to obtain a divorce from her first husband, Lewis Robards, in the state of Tennessee even though he had abandoned her many years before.

Women gained the right to vote less than one hundred years ago. They continue to struggle to gain full membership in "We the people" but have made significant strides. The candidacies of Hillary Clinton for President in 2016, Geraldine Ferraro and Sarah Palin as Vice Presidential candidates in 1984 and 2012 respectively were historic and symbolic moments in the quest for equality of women as part of "We the people".

Today new groups continue to seek inclusion: gays, immigrants from all over the world who do not fit the mold of white Anglo-Saxon Christian heritage, the poor and the homeless.

Compromise

The Constitution itself was a compromise in how our government can operate. The original document was the Articles of Confederation which proved to be unworkable. Then delegates met in Philadelphia in 1787 to write a new document. Within it are more compromises.

The delegates couldn't agree on how the states should be represented, so they set up the House based on population, and the Senate based on state equality with two from each state but having only one vote from each state. This is called the Great Compromise. This Compromise also included the ill-conceived method of counting slaves as 3/5 persons for purpose of representation.

18

The principle of compromise, which was so important in writing our foundational documents, has been ignored in our political system over the past thirty years, as if to compromise is a sign of weakness. Its substitute is an ideological rigidity that prevents anything from getting done in Congress most of the time. In the 1950's Senators BarryGoldwater and John Kennedy opposed each other on the Senate floor but dined together later. This is not happening today.

There is a growing group of people who think that the Constitution must be strictly interpreted to mean what the writers intended. It has been amended 27 times, changing the meaning of the original document in most cases by adding freedom for more people. The first ten amendments, called the Bill of Rights, ratified in 1791, included the five rights in the first amendment, right to trial by jury in the fifth, and states' rights in the tenth.

Later amendments freed enslaved persons (13th), provided for the direct election of Senators by the people not the state legislature (16th), gave women the right to vote (19th) and the 26th lowered the voting age to 18. One ended the poll tax and other practices that restricted voting rights (15th) and another gave the citizens of our nation's capital the right to vote for President.

Several amendments clarified or changed the process of government by limiting a person to two terms as President, by providing for Presidential succession in case of disability, by changing how the judiciary worked and by changing the date for the beginning of Congressional terms from March to January. The only egregious example of limiting freedom was the one prohibiting alcohol manufacturing and usage but this was later repealed by another amendment.

Do people really oppose these amendments? Unfortunately, yes.

Sen. Jim DeMint (R-SC) "suggested that the federal income tax was unconstitutional. The Constitution, when it was signed, it did not even allow a federal income tax." [16] This leads me to believe that strict constructionists do not think the amendments are part of the Constitution. The founders had the foresight to include the provision of amending it in Article 5, making all the amendments part of the Constitution.

In 2010 Jim Linn, an electrical engineer from San Diego, said that "the Constitution must be interpreted in ways that match his understanding of the Founders' intent. That would mean scrapping a lot of the amendments, he acknowledges, but not Nos. 2, 10, 16 and 17." [17] These amendments pertain to guns, states' rights, income tax, and direct election of Senators.

Are strict constructionists disguising their support for slavery, the subjugation of women, and denial of freedoms of speech, religion, and the press? Are they so woefully ignorant of the Constitution that they don't know what they are talking about? The columnist Leonard Pitts rightfully calls these people "crazies". [18]

History tells us that different understandings of the meaning of the Constitution started almost from the beginning. Alexander Hamilton, James Madison, and John Jay wrote the Federalist Papers in support of the Constitution. They agreed that it was important for the states to be united under this Constitution. After Hamilton became Secretary of the Treasury, he promoted a national bank and manufacturing as the basis of our economy. He wanted the national government to assume the debts of the states for their part in the Revolutionary War. He also favored trade with England, from whom people received many of the ordinary items they used and needed. Hamilton based some of his his policies on the "general welfare" clause in the constitution. I highly recommend the book, *Alexander Hamilton* by Ron Chernow, from which I gained most of my comments here about Hamilton and the early days of the Constitution.

During Washington's second term, strong opposition to Hamilton's policies erupted, especially from Hamilton's former collaborators on the Federalist Papers, James Madison, and Thomas Jefferson. They both believed that the strength of the country depended on agriculture and that states could handle banking. Jefferson and Madison favored France over their former enemy, Great Britain, and they believed Hamilton's views were autocratic and and so called their own views democratic.

There was so much respect for Washington that the two political parties did not fully develop until after he left the presidency. Hamilton and his supporters became known as Federalists. While their opponents are often called anti-Federalists, they preferred to call themselves Republicans, recalling the Reppublic of ancient Rome where citizens participated in government. .

The two main parties today do not, of course, represent the original two parties but rather have developed over the years. In fact, the modern Republican Party started in 1854. To avoid confusion in our history books, the original Republican Party is often referred to as the Democratic-Republican Party. What is important to learn from this discussion is that the Constitution never had a singular understanding of its meaning. When people say they want to return to the original meaning, they are showing ignorance about the history of the Constitution.

Federal Government

There are really two levels of government: national and state. Local governments do not act autonomously and are under the jurisdiction of the state government. Each state government is set up differently.

The national government is called a federal government because it is a federation of the states and has its power and authorities from the states, according to the original documents of our country. Today, however, states no longer operate as autonomous states but are de facto districts of the federal government. I make this claim because we are no longer for the most part loyal to our states. The reasons are that travel is so easy that a person seldom lives his entire life in the same state. Rather he or she travels to other parts of the country for a job or retirement. Instant communication also unites our states and people in a way that blurs our differences.

Vestiges of federation still exist. It is most profoundly seen in various states' rights views and policies. There is still the argument that health care and education, among other issues, should be left in the control of states. While progressives might agree with that in principle, the reality is that our nation is too mobile to be separated by contradictory state laws, especially in the very important areas of health care and education.

The authors of our Constitution began a bold experiment in self-government. They separated the main duties of government into three branches: executive, legislative, and judicial. The legislative branch is the Congress and it makes the laws. The executive branch is the President and his cabinet charged with carrying out the laws passed by Congress. The judicial branch is the court system, headed by the Supreme Court, which enforces the laws.

President

The President and Vice-President are elected by the people through the Electoral College, but the heads of departments and agencies are appointed by the President with the approval of the Senate.

The close advisors to the president make up the Cabinet: the heads of State, Defense, Treasury, Commerce, Interior, Health and Human Services, Homeland Security, Agriculture, Transportation, Energy, Veterans' Afairs and Education.

Agencies include the Federal Bureau of Investigation, Central Intelligence Agency, Environmental Protection Agency, the Social Security Administration, Center for Disease Control, Food and Drug Administration, to name a few.

It is this area of government which politicians and others often attack as too large. The Social Security Administration is funded by taxes which are earmarked for this program and should not be considered part of the general budget.

Congress

The writers of the Constitution established two houses in the legislative branch: the House of Representatives and the Senate. The number of Representatives is based on population so that each has an equal voice. The Senate however consists of two Senators from each state with the result that the two Senators from Wyoming, a small populated state, has as much authority as the two senators in California, who represent millions of voters.

Supreme Court

The Supreme Court in Marbury v. Madison in 1803 established that the Supreme Court has the right to interpret the constitutionality of the laws passed by Congress. Ever since then the Court has been making decisions about laws. I have chosen a few to look at more carefully.

Dred Scott decision

In the middle of the slave trade the United States Supreme Court handed down the landmark decision (7-2 vote) in 1857 in the Dred Scott case. The decision declared that not only was Dred Scott not a citizen but that African-Americans, whether enslaved or free, could not be American citizens and therefore had no civil rights. They were declared to be property of the enslavers. It took the bloodiest war in our history to change that decision which is now widely regarded as the worst decision ever made by the Supreme Court. [19]

In this decision, the Supreme Court held property rights higher than human rights, a mistake with tragic consequences.

Citizens United

In 2010 the Supreme Court decided in the Citizens United case that corporations had the right of free speech that is guaranteed under the First Amendment. In effect this decision declared that a corporation is a person. A corporation is property, not a person. Here is another case of distorting the meaning of property. [20] (see page 73 for background.)

Hobby Lobby case

The Green family, owners of Hobby Lobby, used the Citizens United case as a basis for their argument before the Supreme Court. The Greens claimed that their corporation, as a person, has freedom of religion under the First Amendment, and so should not be required to provide contraceptive health care in their employees' insurance. The Supreme Court ruled in favor of the Green family.

Here's an example of how misguided the Citizens United decision was. A corporation, a legal form of property, is not a person and must not be given rights that belong only to people.[21] This decision has resulted in the creation of SuperPacs which can receive unlimited donations and then disburse them to promote a candidate for public office, mostly for President.

McCutcheon v. Federal Election Commission

In the 2012 campaign, Shaun McCutcheon gave to various political candidates and committees, and wanted to contribute more than the aggregate limit under the Federal Election Campaign Act (FECA). He argued that that FECA's aggregate limits violate his First Amendment rights of association and expression. [22]

Mr. McCutcheon, while not challenging the base limits, makes this simple argument: since he is limited to contributing a modest amount to any single candidate, an amount which Congress itself found to be non-corrupting, on what basis may the government limit the total number of contributions he can make? [23]

Money is property. While there is a popular phrase that says, "money talks", the reality is that it is the person who has the money who is talking. The Court in this case is being asked to give free speech rights to property or give more free speech rights to those who have more property. This situation is always a dilemma in a democracy but it makes no sense to give freedom of speech to money!

In 2013 Michigan State Sen. Arlan Meekhof introduced Senate Bill 661 in the Michigan Senate that would double the allowances for contributions in political campaigns. It was signed into law by Gov. Rick Snyder as Public Act 252. It doubles campaign donor limits from $3,400 to $6,800 for candidates for statewide office, from $1000 to $2,000 for candidates for state Senate, and from $500 to $1,000 for candidates for the state House. [24] While there is no argument over free speech rights in this case yet this is an example of those with more money having the ability to use their property to enhance their free speech.

It is hard to believe that the Supreme Court is interpreting the Constitution in a way that does not promote personal liberty but rather corporate interests. At the heart of all American values is the individual who has a high interest in the common good of all. The above decisions, pending cases and laws subvert that personal freedom. What will it take to reverse these latest trends in giving property the status of person with rights that belong only to people and citizens?

State and local governments

Every state also has a Constitution which establishes how the state government will operate. It also details how local governments will work. The executive branch in all states is headed by a Governor. In Michigan he is elected with a Lietuenant Governor. These two are equivalent to President and Vice-President at the federal level.

The legislative branch in Michigan consists of two houses, the same as the federal, but they are called the Legislature rather than Congress. This duplication of titles however does lead to confusion. Originally in Michigan the Senate was based on geographical areas, but this was determined to be unconstitutional by the US Supreme Court in a decision known as the "one man, one vote" ruling.

At my home in Midland Michigan, I live in the Fourth U. S. Congressional District, the 98th State House District and the 36th State Senate District.

State courts

State courts are under the jurisdiction of each state government. A long cherished value in this country is the independence of the judges and the court system. Various ways have been tried to assure this independence. In Michigan judges run for election on a non-partisan ballot. Even though the candidates are nominated by a political party, that party is not shown on the ballot.

In North Carolina the Reppublican legislature has been dismantling the state court system under the guise of reorganizing it to be more efficient. They also are trying to set up court districts that will favor Republicans. In other words, they are gerrymandering the court districts, just like they tried to do in the Congressional districts. However, the United States Supreme Court ruled in May 2017 in a 5-3 decision that Districts #1 and #12 were unsonstitutionally drawn. Justice Elena Kagan said in giving the majority view, "Although States enjoy leeway to take race-based actions reasonably judged necessary under a proper interpretation of the Voting Rights Act, that latitude cannot rescue District 1." [25]

North Carolina had partisan judges in the 1990's but the state changed them to non-partisan. Now the legislature has made them partisan again.

In 2017, the North Carolina legislature reduced the size of the appeals court by three seats. Two of them just happened to be held by Republicans and would be replaced by appointees of the Democratic Governor Josh Stein. Anne Blythe reported, "They decreased the number of emergency judges by nearly 70 percent and cut funding to legal aid organizations that help low-income people. They made a $10 million cut to the state attorney general's office budget." [26] This forced Stein to cut 45 positions and lay off career attorneys.

There is also talk of having the state constitution amended so that all judges could be appointed based on merit. A court redistricting map was shown but neither proposal was acted upon. [27] While in theory these proposals may all sound very democratic or responsible, they are laced with many racist ideas. If these proposals succeed in North Carolina, then that will become a model for other states to follow.

Local Governments

Government jurisdictions can be confusing if one is not attuned to how government works. In Michigan, for example, local governments can be a township, village, city, and county. In addition, the state is divided into various state and federal court districts. Schools are also separate entities and their boundaries cross all of the above named districts. Within each of these, except the courts, are boards, commissions, and agencies.

Is the Government Doing Its Job?

The role of the government is to provide security for the citizens. This is carried out at all levels of government. This security gives us the freedom to move around without fear. It gives us the security of knowing that the drugs the doctor prescribes have been thoroughly researched and will have beneficial effects on us. We have the security of having fresh clean water to drink and play in, clean air to breathe. We have the security of an income in old age or survivor benefits for our family if we die early. We have the security of knowing that diseases are being researched and antidotes developed. We have the security of knowing that prisoners are being responsibly held in confinement. We have the security of health insurance in our old age.

We also have the security of excellent roads and highways which give us the freedom to be mobile in work and play. We also have the security of a universal public school system which ensures an education for all citizens, not just those who can pay for it.   All of these efforts enhance and foster the freedom we all cherish, since no one of us can do these jobs individually. .

Let's take a look at a few examples of how our government is working. The Patriot Act, endorsed by President George W. Bush, allowed Big Brother to check library patrons' book reading. Librarians quickly took up the challenge and destroyed old records, keeping only the record of current books checked out. Also, many refused to give information to the federal government. Local government was acting for our security.

Then Bush decided to intercept emails without legal authorization. He could easily have obtained such authority by going to a special court, but he chose not to take this route, claiming presidential authority granted under the Constitution. He assured us that only international emails were being checked for patterns of communication. Even though some people expressed outrage, this assurance seemed to mollify the critics.

Bush then requested records of millions of telephone calls soon after 9/11/01. AT&T, Verizon, and Bell South complied with the government's request. The U.S. telecommunications industry can handle hundreds of billions of telephone calls each year. Intelligence analysts are seeking to mine these records to expose hidden connections and details of social networks, hoping to find signs of terrorist plots in the vast sea of innocent contacts. By 2006, nearly 2 trillion had been collected since late 2001; only the phone numbers were collected, not names or messages. The National Security Agency is using a program to find patterns of phone calls and find those made to known terrorists. [28] President Bush assured us that ordinary citizens have nothing to fear. Are we led to believe that there are millions of terrorists running around this country making phone calls?

The Bush administration asked for and received data on the searches made by private citizens on the internet. Yahoo complied with the request, but Google refused.

When the Terri Schiavo case was being debated in Florida, President Bush and Congress stepped in to keep Schiavo on a feeding tube.

A family of five bought a house in Black Jack, Missouri, but they discovered a city ordinance required an occupancy permit. The town said it is trying to prevent over crowding. The permit was denied because the man and woman were not married, even though they had been living together for thirteen years and two of the children were theirs. They are not considered family by the city. The city is reviewing the ordinance.

In late June 2006, the Commission on the Future of Higher Education released its proposal to set up a national database that would track the courses taken by college students and their successes and failures throughout their college careers. Data would be linked to individual social security numbers. There was much opposition expressed in an opinion poll and by various people in education. Some worried about security and others wondered how soon this would trickle down to high school and elementary school students. [29]

When the book *1984* by George Orwell first came out, it was generally believed that the liberals of this country would be the ones to take the path of making government into Big Brother. After all, the widely held view was, and is, that it is the liberals that continue to make government bigger and bigger! They are the ones who try to regulate everything, so the thinking goes.

"Surprise, surprise!", as Gomer Pyle used to say. The conservatives are the ones reaching into our private lives breaking the Fourth Amendment rights of protection from capricious searches.

One area where the government is not doing a good job rests with Congress, who fail year after year to balance the budget and allow the national debt to soar.

I have outlined in this chapter the foundation of our form of government and the framework within which our elected representatives must function. The key to effective, efficient, and responsible government is to elect people with integrity. This means that people who do not agree with each other will listen to each other and compromise where possible in order to do their job. I have shown where our government leaders have made mistakes and quite frankly have failed. But the ultimate failure lies with the voters who must take the challenge to vote responsibly.

3. Freedom

People came to America from the very beginning and even now to be free from tyrannical rule, free to worship as they pleased, and free to start a new life. Freedom was a theme of the American Revolution, as expressed in the famous saying of Patrick Henry, "Give me liberty or give me death".

The Preamble to the Constitution says it was written so all people can have "life, liberty, and the pursuit of happiness." The Constitution describes what these words mean in relation to government. The first citizens wanted freedom spelled out in more detail and so the Bill of Rights (the first ten amendments) was added before the Constitution would be approved by the various states.

The First Amendment says, "Congress shall make no law respecting an establishment of religion, or prohibiting the free exercise thereof; or abridging the freedom of speech, or of the press, or the right of the people peaceably to assemble, and to petition the Government for a redress of grievances." These rights are all subject to interpretation, but none is absolute.

The First Amendment Center conducts a survey every year on the people's knowledge of the First Amendment. The Center discovered some astounding results in the survey of 2007. For example, a majority of the respondents could name only one of the rights mentioned in the First Amendment. Only three percent could name all five. Nearly two-thirds said our nation's founders intended the United States to be a 'Christian nation'. There is no mention of Christianity in the Declaration of Independence nor in the Constitution.

These freedoms are in jeopardy in our country because of citizen ignorance and a man who would rather be a demogogue than a President. President Trump has criticized the media all during his campaign and over a year into his presidency for reporting "fake news." He finally in October 2017 called for the Senate to investigate media outlets and look into the possibility of revoking licenses. [30] Poll at that time showed that "46 percent of registered voters believe major news organizations fabricate stories about" Trump and only "37 percent of Americans think the mainstream media does not invent stories." "28 percent of Americans think the federal government should have the power to revoke the broadcast licenses of major news organizations if it says they are fabricating news stories about the president or the administration. Only 51 percent think the government should not be able to do that." [31]

In this same poll, 46 percent of Republicans think the government should have the power to revoke licenses if it says stories are false. This view is right out of George Orwell's book, *1984*, except this is real and that was a novel.

These opinions support the old adage that if you say something loud enough and often enough, people will eventually believe it. In addition, these polls show that the freedoms our ancestors fought so hard for are not important to many people today. If we don't protect these freedoms, then we shall surely lose them, even if they are written into law. We need to have a renewed effort at learning civic rights and duties. We must confront these attacks on our freedoms before it is too late.

Sen. Ben Sasse (R-Neb.), sums it up this way, "The First Amendment is the beating heart of the American experiment, and you don't get to separate the freedoms that are in there," he said this summer [2017]. "You don't have religion without assembly. You don't have speech without press. We all need to celebrate all five of those freedoms, because that's how the 'e pluribus unum' stuff works." [32]

Besides the attack on the freedom of the press, there is an attempt to use freedom of religion to impose religious beliefs and practices and to interpret opposition as an attack on freedom of religion.

Over the two plus centuries of our existence as a nation, we have experienced the growth of freedom in several ways. Enslaved people were set free. Women have secured the right to vote and other civil rights. The voting age has been lowered to 18. Races are allowed to intermarry. Gays are free to marry. The struggle for these freedoms has often involved religious beliefs that opposed the increased freedom. That is still true today.

In the 16th century Christians believed that slavery was morally acceptable, based on Leviticus 25:44-45 which says very clearly that a man can own a slave as property but slaves must be from other nations or from the aliens in their midst.

In Genesis 24:2-4 Abraham is instructed to get a wife for Isaac from among the Hebrews. This is interpreted by some to mean that interracial marriage is forbidden. These are cultural rules for the Hebrew people and have no relevance today. Thus, most people do not support slavery or oppose interracial marriage.

The right to feedom of religion was a struggle in itself. Many of the first European immigrants in the 17th century came for religious freedom but then turned right around and prevented others from having religious freedom. For example, Roger Williams was banned from Massachusetts for his religious beliefs and so set up the colony of Rhode Island. By the time the Constitution was written, religious freedom was a very important right and was included in the First Amendment.

A discovery of the survey by The First Amendment Center in 2007 is that only a little more than half the respondents believe that freedom of religion applies to all religions. The First Amendment is very broad and does not limit the freedom of religion in any way.

Let's look at some aspects of freedom of religion.

Prayer in Public Schools

While this is not a prominent issue in 2018, it does come up from time to time. In the 2007 survey, 58% of respondents favored teacher led prayers in public schools. As a former public school teacher, I have thought about prayer in school for a long time and wondered what people thought about it so I conducted a very unscientific opinion poll. I asked this question, "If you were a teacher in a public classroom, what prayer would you use in such a situation?"

A Muslim man wrote "If the Prayer refers to the Almighty as "GOD", I can tell you that Muslims will be supportive of such prayers." A Hindu woman wrote "I think prayer to a higher force is a wonderful thing for children to learn. It teaches them that somebody other than a human must have created nature, and the oceans, and the beautiful creatures that share the Earth with us. It also teaches us to respect the different ways people pray to this higher force." Even though this is a general comment that could seemingly be applied universally, it would not meet the requirements of the Muslim.

A Jewish man wrote "I guess the easiest way would be to use a completely non-denominational prayer". He gave an example but then went on to say that he would have to take into account the composition of the class, the circumstances of the prayer, and the law or policy that allowed or required the prayer.

An atheist wrote emphatically that prayer is not allowed in school as it would be equivalent to establishing a religion, contrary to the First Amendment. He did go on to say however that "A time of silence, in which children and teacher are free to think whatever they wish, is acceptable to me." Interestingly enough this is exactly what they do in Oklahoma. My teacher friend there wrote "Our state mandates one minute of silence at the beginning of every school day. Some children appear to pray, some work on morning seatwork or homework, read, or attempt to visit. I play supervisor. Students are excused for religious practice reasons."

Another person who has no religious affiliations suggested a humanist prayer that says, "We give thanks for the freedom to think, and to express our thoughts." While that phrase might be acceptable to all religions, the prayer also included thanks for "the freedom to reject inspired books filled with cruelty" that I doubt would satisfy the needs of any religious believer other than perhaps the atheist.

While those of us who profess religious belief might think it is a good thing to have prayer in the public schools, very practical questions arise: whose prayer? which prayer? whose God? Can God be addressed as Higher Force? Creator? Trinity?

Religion and Politics

Let us now turn to a discussion of religion and politics. In 2008 two Republicans were running for President with religion as a factor. Mitt Romney had to assure voters of his Mormonism and Mike Huckabee was and is driven by his Baptist religion in which he is an ordained minister. Barack Obama faced detractors because of his Muslim-sounding name even though

he was never a Muslim, much less a radical one, and has been a Christian
since 1991. This campaign reminded me of previous issues with religion.

John F. Kennedy faced objection to his Catholicism in 1960. Some
people questioned Vatican influence in his decision making. He faced the
objections head on by telling the Houston Area Ministerial Association that
he would make decisions based on national interest "and without regard to
outside religious pressures". He further said that "when my office would
require me to either violate my conscience or violate the national interest,
then I would resign the office". [33]

Since 1960 fundamentalist and evangelical Christians (commonly called
the "religious right") have made a concerted effort to make our country
Christian in their mold. The first openly evangelical Christian President was
Jimmy Carter who was elected in 1976. While Carter did not hide his faith,
he did not use it exclusively to make policy decisions. He has since distanced
himself from the fundamentalist Southern Baptist Christians who are his
religious tradition.

In 2004 another Catholic was running for President. This time various
Catholic Church leaders spoke out against John Kerry because he wasn't
Catholic enough. National interest was not the concern of these outspoken
critics but only that Kerry opposed abortion but not Roe v. Wade.

George W. Bush in 2003 told Mahmoud Abbas, "God told me to strike
at al Qaida and I struck them, and then he instructed me to strike at Saddam,
which I did, and now I am determined to solve the problem in the Middle
East". [34] This is far worse than the Pope giving advice. We can question the
Pope. God's conversations are private.

No Mormon has been elected President so Romney faced the kind of
questioning that Kennedy faced nearly fifty years earlier. Romney told a
select group of supporters at the George Bush Presidential Library in Texas
"A person should not be elected because of his faith nor should he be
rejected because of his faith". [35] Like Kennedy, he then distanced himself
from undue religious pressure in making decisions.

Mike Huckabee, former governor of Arkansas is an Evangelical
Christian and ordained Baptist minister. In contrast to Kennedy, Kerry, and
Romney, he boasts about his faith. He says on his website [36] "My faith
doesn't influence my decisions, it drives them". This is a far different
approach to the relationship between a candidate's religion and how that will
influence his decisions and policies. It makes sense. How important is a
person's faith if it doesn't influence their actions? On the other hand
Huckabee used his religion to win the primary vote in Iowa in 2008. I don't
think that is a healthy mix of faith and politics.

In 1998 when Huckabee was Governor of Arkansas he said to a
gathering of Baptist preachers, "I got into politics because I knew

government didn't have the real answers, that the real answers lie in accepting Jesus Christ into our lives". [37] When he was recently asked about this statement, Huckabee "did not retreat "from it.[38]

We know his faith guides his positions. For example, he is adamantly opposed to abortion and he supports a Constitutional Amendment declaring marriage as a union between one man and one woman. This is clearly an anti-homosexual position based on his faith. Much to his credit, he also is pushing for more concern and care for the poor. This belief, too, stems from his faith.

What concerns me most is Huckabee's stance that the solution to problems in our country is "accepting" Jesus Christ. I can imagine from my conversations with evangelicals that the rest of this statement is "accepting Jesus Christ as my Lord and Savior". Non-Christians might accept Jesus' message, as did Ghandi, but not accept him as Lord and Savior. Accepting Jesus Christ would be tantamount to establishing Christianity as the religion of this country - a violation of the First Amendment. At the very least Huckabee's faith would blur the separation between church and state. Freedom of religion applies to all people.

Muslims

Throughout all of American history there has been rejection of new people who immigrated here. The Irish Catholics were ostracized from society for various reasons when they first arrived in the mid-nineteenth century mostly because they were Catholic. Asians were rejected because they looked different as did people from south of the border. In our time and place Muslims and those from the Middle East are feared.

A *Time* poll in 2010 revealed that 28 percent thought that Muslims should not serve on the Supreme Court and nearly a third thought a Muslim should not be allowed to be President. [39] While these are opinions, they reveal ignorance.

The First Amendment of the US Constitution guaranteeds religious freedom to all people, not just Christians. This understanding of the First Amendment goes back to our founders. George Washington, Ben Franklin, and Thomas Jefferson were all clear that the "freedom of religion" clause included people of all religions including Islam, not just Christianity, as some today would have us believe.

George Washington wrote to the Jews of Rhode Island, that "a Government which to bigotry gives no sanction, to persecution no assistance -- but generously affording to All liberty of conscience, and immunities of citizenship".

In 1784 Washington was concerned only about whether his employees were "good workmen", not whether they were from "Asia, Africa, or

Europe". He then specifically said they "may be Mahometans [Muslims], Jews, or Christian of any Sect -- or they may be Atheists". Ben Franklin wrote that "even if the Mufti [Imam] of Constantinople were to send a missionary to preach Mohammedanism [Islam]to us, he would find a pulpit at his service". "Thomas Jefferson, who owned and read a copy of the Quran, wrote in 1816, 'The most sacred of the duties of a government [is] to do equal and impartial justice to all its citizens'."[40]

Mosque in New York

In 2010 Muslims planned an Islamic community center and mosque near Ground Zero but faced serious opposition.

The 2010 *Time* poll found that "61 percent of respondents oppose the construction of the Park51/Cordoba House project, compared to 26 percent who support it. More than 70 percent concur with the premise that proceeding with the plan would be an insult to the victims of the attacks on the World Trade Center." Many felt it would be an insult to those who lost their lives on 9/11/01. [41]

A Washington Post-ABC News poll, conducted August 30-September 2, 2010, found that "Two-thirds of those polled object to the prospective Cordoba House complex near the site of the former twin towers, including a slim majority who express strongly negative views. Eighty-two percent of those who oppose the construction say it's because of the location, although 14 percent (9 percent of all Americans) say they would oppose such building anywhere in the country." [42]

The *Time* poll also showed that about two thirds opposed the project because they thought "the plan would be an insult to the victims of the attacks on the World Trade Center". Yet, this opinion ignores the fact that as many as sixty American Muslims were killed in that attack. For example, Salman Hamdani, a police cadet and part-time ambulance driver, died "doing everything he could to help those in need" at Ground Zero. [43] [3]

Former Speaker of the House and Presidential wannabe Newt Gingrich said, "The folks who want to build this mosque, who are really radical Islamists, … don't have any interest in reaching out to the community. They're trying to make a case about supremacy." [44]

Then he compared this proposal to the Nazis having a memorial near the Holocaust Museum, a very disturbing comparison. The Nazis were the ones

---

[3] For a partial list of Muslims killed on 9/11 see:http://islam.about.com/blvictims.htm This list includes names of thirty Muslims.

who conducted the holocaust whereas only a tiny radical group of Muslims were responsible for the attack on 9/11.

Gingrich's opinion is not supported by facts. The builders of the Park51/Cordoba House project, which includes a mosque, are Sufi Muslims, the mystical tradition in Islam. Muslims already gather at the site for worship and for cultural understanding. The building has been declared a landmark so any changes were subject to New York landmark designation laws and rules.

The opposition appears to be about demonizing a whole group of people for the actions of a few. The opposition is being bankrolled in part by people like the billionaire Koch brothers. [45]

This is an example of the racist view that holds that if an individual of the white race does something bad, it is an individual act, but if a Muslim (or black, or any other non-white person, commits an evil act, it is indicative of the whole group. This racist view was prevalent in colonial America as early as the 1600's.

Religious Freedom Restoration Act

The federal Religious Freedom Restoration Act of 1993 ensured that interests in religious freedom are protected. By 2015 twenty-one states had passed a state version of the federal law. After the law was passed in Indiana and Arkansas, there was an immediate firestorm of protest by business leaders and others.

In 2016 North Carolina and Mississippi passed similar laws with strong protest from corporate leaders. In Georgia these corporate leaders succeeded in getting the governor to veto the legislation there. I find it interesting that corporations are promoting freedom more than churches.

In response to that backlash, Tim Wildmon, President of the American Family Association, said, "Every American, regardless of political or religious views, should be free to live and work according to their conscience without fear of punishment and backlash from the government. Regardless of what advocates of homosexual behavior say, our government was formed to be freedom's greatest protector, not its greatest threat." [46]

Micah Clark, executive director of the AFA of Indiana explained that conservatives should oppose any effort to clarify that the law does not legalize discrimination. "That could totally destroy this bill." [47]

These two statements make clear that the intent of the law is to discriminate against gays even though the proponents couch the law in religious freedom language.

Let's be clear that the religious freedom the proponents are speaking of is that of Christians, not Muslims, Hindus, Unitarians, Buddhists, and Jews, or any other non-Christian religious group. Unfortunately, the bishops of my Catholic Church support this law and the discrimination it allows.

Jesus Served All People

The origin of this law can be found among Christians, so I invite you to take a look at how Jesus treated people. Jesus entered into a conversation with a Samaritan woman at a well in violation of Jewish law on two counts. Jesus, a male Jew, was not supposed to be alone with a woman. Secondly, Jews were to have nothing to do with the despised Samaritans. Yet Jesus spoke freely to this woman. (John 4:1ff)

Jesus healed the Gerasene Demoniac (Luke 8:26), a Canaanite woman's daughter (Mt 15:22 and Mark 7:26), ten lepers (Luke 17:13-15) and he even touched a leper (Mt 8:3). These acts are all remarkable because he didn't ask first if they were Jews nor did he shun the lepers who were supposed to live apart from the community. In other words he violated Jewish law to achieve a greater good: love of his fellow humans.

The most telling healing relevant to the topic at hand can be found in Luke 7:1-10 and Mt 8:6-8. Both passages discuss the healing of a Roman centurion's servant. This in itself is remarkable because the Romans were the despised occupiers.

The Greek word used in Luke is *doulos* (servant) and in Matthew *pais* (boy). This servant was not just an ordinary household or farm worker, he was "precious" to the centurion. That description is omitted in the New American Bible and is translated in the New International Version as "whom his master valued highly", and in the Revised Standard Version as "who was dear to him". The implication is compelling. Use of pais in Matthew is even more telling because pais means "boy", not servant nor son. Both words suggest a love relationship existed. Jesus extended his compassion without question.

Jesus did not discriminate against serving people because they were different or did not meet his religion's standards. We Christians would do well to go back to the model of Jesus for our daily living. One leader who is doing exactly that is Pope Francis. My book, *Jesus and Pope Francis*, is an attempt to show how Pope Francis is modeling Jesus today.

Possible Outcomes of this Law

Let's look at the implications of this legal discrimination based on religious freedom. What is to prevent a business owner from denying service or products to people of a different color or religion or race? There is much animosity towards immigrants, especially those from Mexico and Central America and those from the Middle East. How big a step would it be for business owners to refuse service to those people using their religion-based conscience?

There is much animosity toward Muslims and all people from the Middle East on the part of some of our national leaders, most notably Donal Trump. He proposed barring all Muslims from entering the United States because some terrorists claim to be Muslim. He actually tried to do that after he was elected, but the courts ruled that his ban was unconstitutional.

The Religious Freedom Restoration Act is a distortion of freedom and the rights guaranteed under the First Amendment. It allows people to discriminate in the name of religion. That is unacceptable. Freedom is for all people, including those who look or believe differently than you or I.

Abortion and Contraceptives

Since abortion is legal in this country, it should be included in health care so that women who need an abortion can get one under the best medical conditions. The same is true for contraceptives. They are totally legal and must not be barred from insurance coverage. Some employees of a religious institution may not be members of the religion and so their freedom is restricted by not having these provisions in their health care. If an institution is only for the benefits of a particular religion, then it can provide whatever benefits it wishes.

Creationism and evolution

Another issue involving religion is creationism. Some people insist that it should be taught in the public schools, but creationism is a religious belief based on one interpretation of creation in the book of Genesis. To appreciate the argument, I believe we must take a look at the meaning of faith and then evolution.

Faith is very much the opposite of science. Faith is acceptance as truth something that cannot be proven. It is very real, but it is based on experience rather than the physical world. We have faith on a purely human level, when we say "I have faith in you" to a friend who is undergoing some struggle in life. Faith jumps to a higher level when we say we believe in a Being that is beyond our physical reach, whom we normally call God. The human understanding of God is so shrouded in anthropomorphic terms that it is hard to distinguish between what is being said about God because we are human and who God really is.

Science, on the other hand, is based on factual evidence and interpretation of those facts can be interpreted using analysis as well as accepted scientific theory to draw conclusions. That's why scientists continue to do research, and why scientific discoveries continue to happen.

We people have numerous beliefs that flow from our faith in God (or lack thereof). One of the Christian expressions of our faith in God is faith that the Bible is the Word of God. There is nothing in the Bible that even remotely suggests that God made a list of writings that belong in the Bible and said that He was the author of them. Our belief in the Bible as the Word of God comes from a declaration of bishops in the 4th century (a more definitive list came later). Before then, the Bible did not exist! So the reference to "scriptures" in 2 Timothy (written in the second century) is a reference to the Hebrew Scriptures, the Christian Old Testament. Even today there is nowhere near unanimity on what writings belong in the Bible.

Even though we refer to the Bible as a "book", it is actually a compilation of numerous books of various literary styles and forms, written over a period of one thousand years. None of the books of the Bible is history, as we think of history, even though many of them refer to historical events. Much of the first eleven chapters of the book of Genesis is myth, a story told to convey a message, in this case religious truth about God or humans.

No one was present at the creation of the world with a pen and pad of paper or a tape recorder. The first chapter of Genesis tells the story of creation in six days, but in chapter two there is quite a different story of creation. Which one is true to what really happened? It doesn't matter, because both stories stem from different sources of hundreds of years of oral tradition and each conveys a beautiful message that God created the world and human beings. Both of these stories are myth.

Evolution is a scientific theory that purports to explain the many varieties of species and life on this planet and how they came to be. It has nothing to do with the origin of the world because science is not about ultimate realities. It is about what can be seen, analyzed, dissected (sometimes) and tested. It has to do with this world as we sense it. Evolution is a scientific theory. As such it should be taught in the science classroom. Creationism is not science nor is intelligent design. These two subjects do not belong in the science classroom. They shouldn't even be taught in the public schools at all, because they are based on faith, except in an overview of religion or religious history.

As a Christian, I don't believe in the literal interpretation of myths, but I am quite fascinated that the days of creation show a progression in the complexity of life over the six days, not quite the same as the scientific theory of evolution, but evolving nonetheless. Even the ancient writers knew somehow that life evolved from the simple to complex. As a person of faith, I believe that there is a God who created the world and all that is in it, but I leave the details to God.

Can faith and science come together in an amicable way? Absolutely. Reconciling the two is the duty of parents, not the job of the public school teachers. For more information on the subject, I suggest *Are Faith and Science Compatible: A Conversation with Teens and Young Adults* by Jerome (Jerry) Klosowski.

Freedom is a core value in this country. Patrick Henry eloquently expressed this in a speech on March 23, 1775, "Give me liberty or give me death." Much of this chapter was about religious freedom, but in 2017 President Trump wants some media outlets shut down because they are reporting "fake news". Who is to judge that their news is fake? Do people want a Hitler type President? The freedom of the press is a fundamental right in this country, guaranteed under the First Amendment.

Freedom is not merely a concept, nor a theory, but a daily lived experience. When daily experiences are curtailed, there is a loss of freedom. When opportunities are cut off because of racism, sexism, xenophobia, or for any other reason, then freedom is lost to those individuals. When one person loses freedom, we all lose freedom. The challenge is to safeguard all freedoms of all people, not just one's own freedom.

4. All Lives Have Dignity

To be "pro-life" one must support all life, not just the lives of the unborn. Somehow politicians, anti-abortion advocates, and many preachers have co-opted the meaning of that sound bite to be very limited.

Somehow capital punishment and killing people in war are not considered anti-life. Somehow a candidate for President can get blackballed by his church because he isn't strongly enough opposed to abortion.

Somehow a President who has "presided over 152 executions, more than any other governor in the recent history of the United States" [4] while Governor of Texas can be called a pro-life President. This same President, however, initiated an ill-advised war that has killed tens, if not hundreds, of thousands of people in Iraq, not to mention the tens of thousands of American dead and wounded. This same war has caused the displacement of millions. This president, of course, was George W. Bush. This recent history is worth remembering becausewe must not repeat it.

"Pro-life" means helping new mothers and children in need, improving access to health care for all people, and raising the educational opportunities of all citizens. It means expanding health care to children under the Children's Health Insurance Program (CHIP). President Trump and the Republicans in Congress defunded CHIP in 2017 and removed the individual mandate in the Affordable Care Act. This latter will leave millions of people without insurance and many small hospitals in rural areas will close, leaving no health care providers nearby. Pro-life means much more than overturning Roe v. Wade.

I believe that for us as a country to have a meaningful discussion about life, we must agree that all human life has intrinsic value, regardless of race, color, education, religion, imprisonment, or any other characteristic one can add to the human species. This value of human life is enshrined in our founding documents in the statement that everyone has the right to life, liberty, and the pursuit of happiness. This is a principle applicable to all people. When we limit that right to certain people, then we diminish the value of that statement and the beauty of our country and what it stands for.

If we value all life, then a conversation can proceed from that. We can then figure out the best ways to solve life problems and provide aid for those situations which impede life through no fault of one's own or even to provide a second chance. We desperately need that conversation today.

---

[4] Sr. Helen Prejean, *Death in Texas* as reported in a *New York Times* book review January 13, 2005

http://www.nybooks.com/articles/17670

The usage of the phrase "pro-life" most likely conjures up Right to Life, an organization most known for its efforts to overturn Roe v. Wade, the United States Supreme Court decision in 1973 that allows women to obtain a legal abortion. Right to Life, along with many religious groups, holds that a fetus is a human person and having an abortion is tantamount to killing a child – murder. The group tells us that more than 50 million abortions have been performed in the United States since 1973. That is without doubt horrendous. On the good news side, abortions in Michigan have declined since 1988. In January near the anniversary of the Rove v. Wade decision, thousands march on Washington and other places to urge the overturn of this decision.

The right to life extends beyond the womb to include decent housing, adequate food and clothing, access to a good education and proper health care, especially pre- and post-natal care. The way we as a society ensure these rights for everyone is certainly subject to debate, discussion, and compromise, but the solutions must enhance life, not take it away by depriving people of basic human rights.

There are said to be 47.6 million people living in poverty in 2014 [48] up from 30 milion just a few years ago. Poverty is a right to life issue. 21 percent of those under age 18 live in poverty while only ten percent of those over age 65.

In the book *The End of Poverty* by Jeffrey Sachs, I read that 15,000 people die every day in Africa from diseases that could be prevented by drugs and treatment now available to us. People in other countries have the right to life also. Worldwide, nine million people die each year from these same diseases or, worse yet, from starvation. We have plenty of food in our world to satisfy all who are hungry.

Murder is a chilling word that people use regarding abortion. I like to apply that word to state sponsored executions also. Quite often, however, someone will object. They seem to think there are exceptions to the commandment that says, "Do not kill". They think that a criminal about to be executed has lost his/her right to life. I say the executioners are the ones who have lost human dignity. Criminals have a right to life too.

Let's put war under the framework of right to life. The war in Iraq caused the death of hundreds of thousands of Iraqis with one estimate as high as 655,000. The Iraq Study Group reported that 1.6 million Iraqis were homeless and 1.8 million Iraqis have fled the country. Many of those still living there are in desperate situations, wondering if their "good-bye" in the morning will be the last one. Over 4,000 Americans have died and thousands were injured in this war. In 2015, Iraq is still anunstable country and is an ISIS stronghold. War is a right to life issue too.

For me, abortion, poverty, execution, and war are all life issues. I recognize that the application of this right to issues other than abortion is subject to debate and compromise. I realize there are arguments on both sides, but I suggest we approach all these issues from the value of life before we enter into compromise on specifics of housing, education, health care, execution, poverty, imprisonment, and war. Perhaps that focus will lead us in a better direction in dealing with these issues.

The Unborn

The underlying questions surrounding abortion involve the beginning of life. Is there a new human life at the time when the sperm and egg unite (that is, at conception)? Or does it begin when the zygote implants in the wall of the uterus, up to twelve days later? If a woman uses the so-called morning after pill, is that really an abortion?

The real question seems to me to be when that mass of cells becomes a human being rather than just the potential to be a human being. It cannot be based on genetic makeup because the fertilized egg could divide and become two or three with the same genetic makeup. It would seem that a human person comes into being after that point.

Let's take an example from the plant world. I don't think anyone would call the acorn a tree although it certainly has the potential to be an oak tree. Is it a tree when the seed inside the shell begins to break open the shell? Or is it when it sprouts beyond the shell? Maybe it is when the new growth takes root.

All analogies are lacking including this one. If taken to the extreme it would be nonsense. But I think there is something to be learned here. Even though it has the potential to be an oak tree, the acorn is nothing but a seed until it takes root. Couldn't the same be said for the zygote in the womb of a woman? Some people have their minds made up in answer to the question when does life begin. Some churches teach that life begins at conception, but not all would agree with that.

The number and percentage of abortions in relation to live births has been decreasing since the early 1980's during both Republican and Democratic administrations. We must be doing something right even though some voices seem to indicate otherwise. About 88 percent of all abortions occur in the first trimester. Less than two percent are performed as a result of rape or to save the life of the mother.

There is one piece of this issue that baffles me and at the same time can offer a compromise toward reducing abortions. Let me give an example. Carrie, Alice and Betty are all six months pregnant. If Carrie gives birth at this point she can save the baby's life by the use of all the advanced technology we have available today, If Betty was shot to death along with her unborn baby, the killer would be charged with two counts of homicide, not one. Alice on the other hand could have her baby aborted. How can the baby in the womb of these three women be considered a human being under some conditions and not a human being in another?

It seems to me to be a no-brainer that there is human life at this stage and must be protected from elective abortion. If that period is five months, not six months, then it should be defined at five months. This contradiction must be eliminated in the law.

The Right to Life movement focuses heavily on overturning Roe v. Wade but that will not solve the problem of abortions. A World Health Organization study showed that countries that went from legal abortions to illegal abortions resulted in greater maternal deaths. A more recent study indicates that even the abortion rate increased when abortion was made illegal. The real problem relating to abortion is the reality that abortion is not the issue, but only a symptom of other issues affecting the woman who wants an abortion. These other issues include the psychological state of the woman, the circumstances surrounding the pregnancy, the knowledge of the woman and the one who made her pregnant, and more. It is time that the man who made the woman pregnant be part of the conversation and responsibility.

Minorities

Abortion is not the only pro-life issue even though many members of Right to Life focus solely on that issue. There are several large groups of people who are denied life because they are part of a minority group that the majority denigrates in some way.

There is only one human race. We are all one human family. We have more in common with each other than we have differences. I was taught there are several human races based on color. It is from this understanding of race that we derive the word racism which is a demeaning attitude or action by one group over another. These groups are generally differentiated by color but ethnicity, origin, and religion are other ways we have separated ourselves from one another. Other words for racism are prejudice, bias, and bigotry.

Given the general usage of the word racism, it is an ugly blotch on our American ideals. It is a hatred toward minorities that has occurred all during our history, beginning with the Native Americans, Irish and Eastern European immigrants, and people from Asia. Mostly, however, the word is used in conjunction with those of African descent or simply, black people. The source of this racism can be found in our history.

In the movie *South Pacific,* there is a particularly poignant moment when Nellie meets Emile DeBecque's children from his first wife. She is very much interested in marrying DeBecque but DeBecque has kept his children from her sight until this moment. With a look of disdain Nellie backs away from him and cannot marry him because the children are brown. DeBecque then sings "You have to be carefully taught" to be prejudiced. Nellie's inability to accept the children came from what she was taught about being white and the privileges that go with that. Let this be the backdrop for what I have to write about divisions in our society.

The *Anatomy of Peace* says, "'If you see people of a particular race or culture as objects … your view of them is racist, whatever your color or lack of color or your power or lack of power." It applies to "all divisions, whether between rich and poor, old and young, educated and uneducated, religious and nonreligious, Catholic and Protestant, Shia and Sunni." [49]

Recently South Carolina Lt. Gov. André Bauer,[5] running for governor on the GOP ticket, likened "the poor to stray animals." And his grandmother taught him not to feed stray animals because "they breed. You're facilitating the problem if you give an animal or a person ample food supply." [50] That's

---

[5] ` Speaking of those who receive public assistance, Bauer recently told an audience, ``My grandmother was not a highly educated woman, but she told me as a small child to quit feeding stray animals. You know why? Because they breed. You're facilitating the problem if you give an animal or a person ample food supply. They will reproduce, especially ones that don't think too much further than that. And so what you've got to do is you've got to curtail that type of behavior. They don't know any better."

racism too. His comments scarcely received public notice, much less criticism.

Many people have called for a dialog on race in this country. Candidate Obama took up this challenge when he delivered a personal and heart felt address in Philadelphia in 2008 on race[51]. Yet, some said he did not do enough and others said he talked about race too much.

Being white in America means being a member of the majority and dominant group and it is more than being white skinned. Thandeka, associate professor of theology and culture, Meadville/Lombard Theological School, shed new light on the issue of racism in studies regarding white identity.[52] There is an identity that goes with being white. For example, a person's natural instinct is to reach out to others without any racial or class considerations. When this instinct is disrupted by parents or other adults who do not want whites associating with other races, there develops a self-betrayal for stifling one's own natural feelings. This self-betrayal is then expressed as disgust for another race. It is not enough to be white but that whiteness must be expressed in separation from black people (or brown, red, yellow for that matter). Adults, too, can stifle natural feelings of affection and thus engender the same self-betrayal.

This white identity becomes so deeply engrained that poor whites do not even recognize their natural solidarity with poor people of other races. Even though both groups share the same condition, whites fail to see it and distance themselves socially as well. As whites grow up, they don't even recognize this characteristic of being white. Thandeka further wrote that this white identity allowed whites socially and legally "to taunt, police, humiliate, mob, rape, lynch, jibe, rob, jail, mutilate, and burn" black people. White identity camouflaged the immorality of these actions. Some of these experiences are dramatically described in a novel called *The Help* (2009) by Kathryn Stockett.

I cannot emphasize enough the point that we white people have been and continue to be the majority in the United States and for the most part make the rules that govern . It is very easy to miss a point of prejudice in our thinking and acting. For example, I firmly believe that much of the opposition to President Obama had more to do with him being a black man than opposition to his policies. And that is racism.

More concrete examples include the many killings of black males by white men in recent years. Just to mention a few, there was the killing of Trayvon Martin in Florida by George Zimmerman, the killing of twelve-year old Tamir Rice in Cleveland by a police officer, the killing of Michael Brown by Darren Wilson in Ferguson, MO, the killing of Freddie Gray in Baltimore, and the killing of a black student in Cincinnati.

The phrase "civil rights movement" has a very clear association with the struggle for equality by black Americans. In contrast, Glenn Beck had billed a rally in front of the Lincoln Memorial on August 28 2010, 47 years to the day after Martin Luther King Jr. famously spoke there, as an effort to "reclaim the civil rights movement".

"'This is a moment,' said Glenn Beck on his radio program, '… that I think we 'reclaim' the civil rights movement. It has been so distorted and so turned upside down. … We are on the right side of history. We are on the side of individual freedoms and liberties and damn it, we will reclaim the civil rights moment. We will take that movement, because we were the people that did it in the first place!'. [53]

Using this phrase is either a display of monumental ignorance of historical fact that the civil rights movement was entirely a struggle by black people for equality or it is a deliberate effort to revise history. In either case Beck's opinions lack credibility and are obscene, as Leonard Pitts wrote. It makes me think that some people believe that if they say something often enough or yell it loud enough, it becomes a fact.

Racist ideas and the very notion of racism is not the result of ignorance. Racist ideas rather perpetuate racism because the ideas are supported by religious leaders, and "economic, political, and cultural self interest," which change over time. [54]

The Civil War may have freed enslaved people from being property but those in power continued to enslave black people through legal discrimination and segregation as well as practices which, though illegal, were not stopped or prosecuted. Ibram Kendi wrote,

> *Someone was lynched, on average, every four days from 1889 to 1929. Often justifying the ritualistic slaughters on a false rumor that the victim had raped a White woman, White men, women, and children gathered to watch the torture, killing, and dismemberment of human beings—all the while calling the victims savages. Hate fueled the lynching era.* [55]

Today in the aftermath of the Civil Rights Acts in the 1960's, new racist ideas have taken hold. Black people and other minorities are still barred from jobs, education, and homes through more subtle actions. The most high profile racist idea was the "tough on crime" policy of Presidents Nixon, Reagan, and Clinton. Police shootings are disproportionately directed at black people.

I have a dream, to paraphrase Dr. Martin Luther King's famous speech, that one-day people will see each other as human beings, regardless of race, gender, religious affiliation, country of origin, ethnicity, or sexual orientation. May that day come soon.

Gays

On June 26, 2015, The United States Supreme Court decided in a 5-4 decision "that the fundamental right to marry is guaranteed to same-sex couples by both the Due Process Clause and the Equal Protection Clause of the Fourteenth Amendment to the United States Constitution." Prior to this decision thirty-six states, the District of Columbia, and Guam already issued marriage licenses to same-sex couples.[56]

This landmark decision raised the debate over homosexuality to a new level. Instead of just arguing against the morality of homosexuality, opponents must now deal with the law.

The word homosexual brings up many emotions because of three letters in that word: s-e-x. Sex is a very troubling subject in the United States and indeed the world. For the most part I think we have a very minimal understanding of sexuality. Much of this is caused by outdated religious teaching. Because of this negative emotional energy surrounding the word homosexual, I prefer to call homosexual people gay, including both men and women.

Gays comprise up to ten percent of the total population but are largely invisible. They are fellow students, co-workers, neighbors and church attendees. They are engineers, chemists, teachers, doctors, nurses and laborers. They are next to us and there is no way we would know it. They have no apparent characteristics like skin color. Their only distinction is that they are attracted to members of the same gender.

When flipping channels one night, I found a program on which a panel of people spoke to various aspects of issues surrounding their lives. The panel consisted of white and black men and women with various professional responsibilities and religious affiliations. They were gays and lesbians speaking about issues affecting them.

The men and women on that TV program experience something that is common to all men and women: love. They love people of the same gender and want to have the freedom to be public about that. The cultural, religious and societal taboos against their freedom to love changed very slowly but this movement toward equality has grown rapidly in recent times and reached recognition in the Supreme Court's landmark decision.

Several years ago some people confided in me regarding the acceptance of gays. Adding personal stories to this discussion helps to eliminate the negative feelings about gays. A couple wrote me:

"Our 19-year old son is gay, which we have known since he was 12. We love and accept him totally and want him to be able to share his life with someone he loves and enjoy the same legal benefits we have as a married couple. It has been hurtful to all of us to live with the discrimination against gays which is so prevalent in our society."

A woman shared this story "about one of the kindest, most sensitive men that I have ever known."

He grew up in a "small" town. The people there were very opinionated and closed minded to "persons of different orientations" than theirs. He grew up, often afraid of what would happen to him if he ran into the children of these closed-minded folks, and he was alone often.

"This young man graduated summa cum laude, has a very responsible position with the US Government and has become a very successful adult. He gives tirelessly to those affected with AIDS, MS, cancer and heart disease. He is non-violent and has learned to keep his lifestyle secret from those in that small town.

"Our family cries when we hear of gay people being "hated, treated like non-humans, banned from relatives' homes, etc."

"This man is my son. He lives in the DC area now and is relatively at peace.

Homosexuality is a hot topic because of the Bible and the interpretation of it by some Christians. Some support completely gay, lesbian, bisexual, and

transgendered people but others find them defying God's laws. A retired
Methodist minister wrote, "My denomination is still haggling over the
acceptance of all people, in spite of the fact that it has adopted as it slogan,
'Open Hearts, Open Minds, Open Doors.'" A phone caller reminded me that
the Catholic Church condemns homosexuality.

Some of the problem with quoting the Bible is that all are using
translations of the ancient Hebrew and Greek texts. A biblical translation is
always an interpretation, usually to support one's religious beliefs. We really
need to study the Bible in its original languages or read commentaries based
on those languages. The context of every book and chapter is also important
to keep in mind when reading the Bible.

One such example is the First Letter to the Corinthians (6:9-10) which is
translated in the New International Version as *"Male prostitutes nor
homosexual offenders"* will enter the kingdom. The New American Bible
however translates the Greek as *"catamites and sodomites"*. A footnote
explains that a catamite was a "boy prostitute" and a sodomite was an adult
man who engaged in prostitution with boys. The meaning is quite different
than the meaning in the NIV. St. Paul is condemning prostitution, not
consensual and loving homosexual relationships.

Leviticus 18:22 says, "For a man to lie with a man as with a woman is
an abomination." It seems very clear but let's take a look at some of the other
prescriptions in that book. Verse 25:44 says that a person may possess slaves,
both male and female, provided they are purchased from neighboring
nations. Verse 11:10, says eating shellfish is an abomination. Verse 21:20
states that I may not approach the altar of God if I have a defect in my sight.
Verse 19:27 forbids a man to get his hair trimmed, including the hair around
his temples, Verse 11:6-8 says that touching the skin of a dead pig makes one
unclean. Verse 19:19 forbids planting two different crops in the same field.
Verse 24:16 forbids wearing garments made of two different kinds of thread.
These verses have nothing to do with sexuality, but no one preaches or
follows these prescriptions either. Why then is verse 18:22 to be upheld?

The book of Leviticus is a "holiness" code for the Hebrew people in
order to set them apart from their neighbors. That is why they had all the
dietary restrictions about fowl, reptiles, and shellfish. Even the other books
of the Hebrew Scriptures (Old Testament) contain prescriptions that applied
only to the Hebrew people.

There was a very special relationship between David, warrior and king
of Israel, and his predecessor's son, Jonathan (1 Samuel 20 & 2 Samuel 1).
Mourning Jonathan's death, David says, "I grieve for you, Jonathan, my
brother; you were very dear to me. Your love for me was wonderful, more
wonderful than that of women." There is some evidence to make one suspect,
if you study this relationship as it is recorded, that this love that David speaks

of was more than platonic. This point is usually ignored or glossed over because the leaders of the Christian Church would not even consider that relationship as anything but friendship.

The interpretation and translation of various words and verses in the Bible to refer to homosexuals is a recent historical phenomenon beginning only about two hundred years ago with the advent of religious fundamenatlism. Prior to that time the words in question were translated differently.[57] [58] Sexual orientation wasn't even known until the mid-nineteenth century.[59]

The use of the famous story of Sodom (Genesis 19) as a denunciation of homosexuals and their activity is not supported even in other places in the Bible. Pride is the evil at Sodom in Ecclesiastes 16:8 and Wisdom 19:13-14. Pride, idleness, and neglecting the poor are mentioned in Ezekiel 16:48-49 as the sin of Sodom. Jesus implied the sin of Sodom was inhospitality in Matthew 10:14-16.

Romans 1:26-27 is part of a list of pagan temple practices that Saint Paul condemns. In 1 Timothy 1:10 the Greek word arsenokoitai is quite rare and probably means "male prostitute".[60] This was the meaning until well into the fourth century.

It is dangerous to read the words of the Bible as literal truth. Exodus (35:2) says those who violate the Sabbath rest should be put to death. Remember the Sabbath is Saturday. I doubt many of us would be alive if this command were carried out! Even Jesus gave commands that are untenable if taken literally. Mark 9:43-49 records Jesus telling us to cut off our hand or arm or pluck out our eyes if they are occasions of sin. Clearly this is not to be taken literally. It is hyperbole.

The Bible has to be understood in context and in its historical development. It did not just appear from the hands of God.

Gay Marriage

I know a number of gay men. Many are in long term relationships ranging from ten to thirty years. They are not different.

Opponents of gay marriage say that allowing gays to marry is an affront to the true meaning of marrage which they interpret as a union of a man and a woman for purposes of companionship, love, and having children. Yet bigamy and polygamy have been part of the marriage tradition longer than the tradition of one man and one woman. This is very clear in the Bible. For some marriage is also a convenience because of laws that favor marriage. Anyone who thinks that marriage is about sexual activity has a very narrow understanding of marriage. Such a marriage is on a weak foundation. For some religious people marriage is the union of a man and woman in a lifelong relationship ordained by God. Some say its primary or even only purpose is the begetting and raising of children.

An argument used against gay marriage is that gays and lesbians cannot beget children. This however is a slap in the face of a heterosexual couple who can't have children for one reason or another. Is their union not a marriage?

Even though marriage is deeply embedded in human tradition and culture, it is a civil contract in the United States that has civl and religious overtones. That is why we have to obtain a "marriage license" in the United States in order to get married. A man and a woman cannot go to a clergy person or public official and get married without that license given by the various states with differing requirements. These may include a waiting period, counseling about marriage, and an expiration if not used within a specified time period.

Separation of church and state is a high priority and ideal in this country. Yet we have blurred that separation when it comes to marriage by allowing marriages witnessed by clergy people to be legal contracts. In other words the consummation of that license is done in a religious ceremony.

With this civil contract comes civil rights. These include filing joint tax return, the right of one to attend the other in the hospital, having health insurance together, the right to inheritance, and favorable estate transfer provisions. A spouse also has the right to retain a home when the other spouse needs to be in a nursing home.   All of these "rights" are civil and not dependent on a religious meaning of marriage.

Separating the civil contract of marriage from the religious ceremony would solve the problem of "gay marriage". Gays and lesbians could marry in a civil ritual that gives them the civil rights of marriage but does not obligate churches to accept or witness such civil marriages. If the gays or lesbians belong to a church that accepts them, then they can ritualize their marriage in a religious ceremony as well. Simple, straightforward, and honest. This is precisely what the Supreme Court has done in its decision to recognize gay marriages.

In 2007 a friend wrote to me,

My partner of five years and I are getting married next weekend. A driving force behind our getting married is to have legal protection for our family. Our twins are due in February and we're grateful for the protections marriage in Massachusetts affords us. My personal regret is that my home state has chosen to make sure that my children have had those legal protections denied by the state constitution. It doesn't make me very comfortable visiting Michigan. But of course, I could never deny my parents seeing their grandchildren."

With the Supreme Court decision, he doesn't have to worry about that anymore.

Billy in Missouri wrote, *"My partner and I have been together 13 years and hope to be able to marry in our lifetime. We are 36 years old so I think there is hope for this to come true."*

Now they can!

Immigrants

Protesting immigration restrictions

Immigrants are another group of people who are shunned as undesirables in this country. They are criticized and accused of all kinds of activities not suitable for our great United States. They are quite often classified as "illegal" but that is incorrect; rather they are undocumented. Let us try to make some sense of this issue, especially in regard to the right to life.

"Give me your tired, your poor,
Your huddled masses yearning to breathe free,
The wretched refuse of your teeming shore.
Send these, the homeless, tempest-tossed to me,
I lift my lamp beside the golden door!"

This is an excerpt from a poem by Emma Lazarus that is engraved beneath the Statue of Liberty. I first heard these words in grade school. They represented the values and high ideals of the United States at one time.

These ideals probably inspired my grandfather, Charles Bufka, to immigrate from Bohemia in 1859, even though the actual writing of these words came later. He worked in Chicago for twenty years before he bought land in Leelanau County, Michigan. He built the house where my father, brothers, and I were born.

I received an email that quoted Theodore Roosevelt's views on immigration in the early part of the twentieth century. He declared acceptance of all the immigrants only with serious provisos: they must be assimilated into the American way of life, speak English, and be loyal only to the flag and the American people. While those ideals make sense, it seems foolish to brand immigrants as criminals if they don't meet these conditions, as some of our leaders are wont to do in today's immigration arguments.

Even though my grandfather became a citizen in 1881, he continued to speak his native language. I wonder if he would have voted for Teddy. My father, too, was fluent in Bohemian while growing up. I often heard him speak to friends and siblings in that language. Did this make him a bad citizen?

I recognize the circumstances of immigration today are much different than they were 100-150 years ago. We then had wide open spaces where immigrants could settle and farm. The U.S. was still a largely agricultural economy, a condition that no longer exists. Cities were also burgeoning with industrialization, however, that needed workers. These immigrants fulfilled that need in many cases. Even so, they were criticized and discriminated against, just as immigrants are today.

Today's immigrants are filling a need also by working in jobs that people already here don't want. By so doing, they are making money and spending it, thus adding to our economy. Because they arrived here under less than favorable circumstances does not mean that the high ideals of America don't apply to them.

In the early 1990's , I saw the movie, *El Norte*, which depicted Enrique and Rosa in their struggle to reach the United States from Guatemala. They were a teenage brother and sister who saw the delights of America in an old Good Housekeeping magazine. Their father was killed after protesting working conditions in their country and their mother disappeared soon after.

The movie tells the story of their passage through Mexico and efforts to get into the US. Roger Ebert said they ended up arriving through a "rat infested drainage tunnel" and their first sight was the "glittering lights of Los Angeles." They found jobs in the illegal marketplace as a waiter and a maid.

The story is told from their perspective, showing their culture and dignity as human beings."

President George W. Bush said in his State of the Union address on January 28, 2008 "Illegal immigration is complicated, but it can be resolved. And it must be resolved in a way that upholds both our laws and our highest ideals." He is right on this one. About eleven million undocumented immigrants are residing and working in this country.

The complication that President Bush referred to rests on four points: 1) This situation did not happen over night. It is the cumulative effect of not paying attention to it for many years.

2) There has been a federal law on the books since the mid-1980's which requires employers to verify that new hires are citizens by completing Form I9. The reality is that this law is neither complied with nor enforced very seriously. Both the government and companies have largely ignored it. A Midland employer strongly objected to my claim that employers ignored Form I9, because she complied.

3) The undocumented people comprise a mixture of spouses, children, and those seeking asylum. They also include those who arrived here legally but have stayed beyond the expiration date of their documents.

4) Michael Kinsley wrote that the phrase "illegal immigrants" is a cop-out and a cover for covert hostility toward all immigrants. [61]

The reality of terrorism has added fear to the situation. Some people are using immigrants as a scapegoat for the loss of jobs.

Some Republicans, including Donald Trump in 2016, periodically rant about these immigrants and vow to deport them if elected president. Trump is setting up an "army" of immigration agents to find and deport immigrants without documents. While it may be expedient to harangue about deportation of all of them, this process would fly in the face of the Fourth Amendment which prohibits unlawful searches. It would also be costly in hiring investigators to find all these people and transporting them out of the country. It would finally be inhumane to send people away from the only place they ever lived. In the case of children, especially those who were born here and are presumed citizens under the Fourteenth Amendment, deportation would be an unconscionable and unconstitutional act. Yet President Trump in August 2017 revoked the executive order of President Obama that allowed young people brought here illegally as children to stay under certain conditions. The revocation affects an estimated 800,000 people who have lived most of their lives nowhere else than the United States. Trump also has begun sending back immigrants who were residing under Temporary Protective Custody(TPC) status because of turmoil in their homeland.

State legislatures, including in Michigan, have introduced various legislation of a punitive nature. Some states have even passed them. Arizona has hiked the penalty for hiring undocumented workers. Oklahoma passed "Taxpayer and Citizen Protection Act of 2007" which makes it "unlawful … to transport" or "conceal, harbor, or shelter from detection" any undocumented immigrant. The Catholic Bishop of Tulsa Edward Slatterly circulated a petition on which he obtained 1500 signatures saying they would not obey this unjust law. The penalty for breaking this law is up to one year in prison or $1,000 fine or both.

In 2011, a new Republican legislature and governor enacted HB 56, the Alabama Taxpayer and Citizen Protection Act. Chief sponsor Micky Hammon warned the undocumented population that he would "make it difficult for them to live here, so they will deport themselves." Renting a house or giving a job to an "illegal" became a crime. Police were empowered to demand proof of citizenship from anyone who looked as if he or she might lack it. School administrators were instructed to do the same to children.[62]

Republicans blamed President Obama for the law not working because the Justice Department sent signs to employers that said no one could deny the right to a job. I remember the Catholic Church opposed the law as well on grounds they wanted to provide help under religious freedom guaranteed in the First Amendment.

I believe the ideals President Bush referred to are summed up in the words at the base of the Statue of Liberty. Our founders declared that all have the "right to life, liberty, and the pursuit of happiness." These high values in our country need to be observed in setting policy for undocumented people.

Along with these ideals is the fact that we are a nation of immigrants. From a Christian perspective it would be well to heed the command to "welcome the stranger in our midst." (See NAB Deuteronomy 10:19 and Matthew 25:43).

Many are saying that this issue must be resolved within the context of overall immigration reform. While I don't disagree with that statement, it should not be used to exacerbate the situation or prolong the solution.

Even though every country has the right to limit the number of immigrants to their country, this issue of undocumented people requires special consideration because of the complications involved. These resolutions must include securing family stability, setting up a temporary worker program, restoring due process protection, legalizing their status and allowing them to obtain citizenship. At the same time the United States must establish just and effective border control.

Let's figure out a way to teach immigrants English and the American way of life and what it means to be a citizen. Let's help them assimilate into our culture without destroying their dignity and traditions. We can't do this by excluding them from an education and other benefits of American society.

We should encourage employers with tax credits for obtaining legal status for their undocumented workers, instead of ignoring them and putting them at risk by unscrupulous employers or government agents.

We need to keep families together. Deportation is not a solution since many of those that would be scheduled for deportation have children born in this country, who are full citizens and therefore entitled to stay here. President Trump is enforcing deportation in defiance of these principles. He had a 39 year old married man deported back to Mexico in January 2018. The man had been here since age 10, married, has two children, had a landscaping job and had committed no crimes.

Yes, the situation is different today than a century or so ago, but the words of President George W. Bush in this regard must be foremost in our discussions and debates: "I know this is an emotional debate, but one thing we must not lose sight of is that we are talking about human beings, decent human beings that need to be treated with respect." (Quoted by Leonard Pitts, Jr.) They are not all rapists, criminals, and thugs, as President Trump wants us to believe.

Victims of Gun Violence

The lives of those killed by gun violence are valuable also. As we continue into the 21st century, this subject becomes more and more important to discuss and resolve.   This is especially true in light of the worst mass shooting in American history on October 1, 2017 in Las Vegas, where 58 people were killed by a lone gunman using military style weapons.

I think we have been framing the debate or discussion on guns too narrowly on the Second Amendment and the right to own and/or regulate guns. Let's just take a moment to look at this issue from a different perspective. I believe without a doubt that the chance of becoming a victim of gun violence is far greater if there are guns available than if there are none available. I hope that we all can agree with that statement. It has nothing to do with the Second Amendment and the usual argument.

I came across this way of looking at the gun issue when I read about the plan to study gun violence by the Center for Disease Control (CDC) in 1995. Rep. Jay Dickey thought this proposed study was a way for the government to control gun ownership and so fought hard to add an amendment on the appropriations bill to prevent the CDC from conducting such a study. The bill also eliminated the $6 million to fund the study. Mark Rosenberg, Professor of Medicine at the University of Minnesota Medical School, testified at a committee hearing for the CDC but his view was rejected.

Twenty years later in 2015 these two men are on the same side in support of a study on gun violence. Dickey has come to see that the continued mass shootings need to be studied so that solutions can be reached. This union did not come about quickly but started nearly twenty years ago when Dickey befriended Rosenberg after the hearings and they gradually became very close friends. [63]

While the following comparison is not totally valid, it does serve a point. The CDC did a study on deaths caused by automobiles and concluded that seat belts save lives. This change in car safety reduced the number of annual deaths in car accidents from about 50,000 to about 30,000, the same number of people as are killed by gunshots, whether intentional or accidental. Gun violence, by the way, is increasing. Given the probability that a shooting is more likely to occur if there are guns available, then it is fair to conclude that we are headed for an exponential increase in gun deaths because of the exponential increase in guns available.

I think it is also fair to say that the more common guns are, then the more common it will be to settle disputes by using guns. It is already legal to openly carry a weapon in many states and some states allow people to carry concealed weapons. Usually the ability to carry a concealed weapon requires a permit and training but a bill introduced in Michigan in 2017 would drop the permit and training requirements. These provisions are all leading to conflicts with guns.

So rather than look at a way to take guns away from people, let's look at the violence caused by the use of guns and figure out how to minimize that violence. According to the Center for Disease Control (CDC), there were more than 38,000 [64] deaths from firearms in the United States in 2016, up from 33,169 in 2013. This total does not include those who were killed legally by police. In 2013 about a third of the deaths were homicides and two-thirds were suicide with the rest being accidental or unknown. In 2013. the deaths by firearms represented 1.3% of all deaths. In addition, firearms were used to cause tens of thousands non-fatal injuries [65] and health care costs involving gunshots were about a half billion dollars in 2013.The number of deaths from firearms averages about 35-40 per day and the number of injuries about 75 per day.

The number of firearms owned by private individuals is more than 300 million but the number of households owning guns is down from a high of 54% in 1977 to 36% in 2016. However, the number of firearms per household has increased from about 4 to 7. [66]

Twenty-seven Americans were killed in gun homicides on Christmas Day 2015, a number comparable to the number of people killed in gun homicides in an entire year in places like Australia or Great Britain. That number was equal to the total number of people killed in gun homicides in an entire year in Austria, New Zealand, Norway, Slovenia, Estonia, Bermuda, Hong Kong and Iceland, combined." [67]

Americans are roughly 20 times more likely to be murdered with a gun than people in other developed countries. Women in our country are roughly 11 times more likely to be killed by a gun than women in other high-income countries. From 2001 through 2012, 6,410 women were murdered in the United States by an intimate partner using a gun – more than the total number of U.S. troops killed in action during the entirety of the Iraq and Afghanistan wars combined.

Every day in our country, eight children and teens are killed by guns. American children are roughly 11 times more likely to die by guns than children in other high-income peer countries.

Statistics on deaths by firearms were collected starting in 1968. These deaths total 1,516,863, compared to 1,396,733 killed in all the wars from the Revolution through the war in Iraq. [68]

Let's put some faces on these numbers. In 2008 Joe Horn shot and killed two men who were robbing a neighbor in Pasadena, Texas. He called 911 and was warned not to intervene but shot the robbers anyway as he became more agitated about the delay in police arrival. He was not charged with any crime. [69]

On Christmas Day 2015, people killed by firearms included the parents of a young child during a robbery in Columbus, Ohio and a young couple in their vehicle in the early morning hours near Augusta, Maine. Shot but not killed was a Texas grandfather, whose 73-year-old wife says she shot him for "continuous marital issues and infidelities." [70]

Two men wre in a verbal argument inside a bar. After they left the bar, one of them shot the other in the leg. A woman at a Home Depot store saw two shoplifters leaving the store, pulled out her gun and shot at the fleeing truck in a parking lot. She hit one or more tires and was charged with the misuse of a firearm.

The President of Liberty University, Jerry Falwell, Jr., urged the students to get permits to carry a concealed weapon and has given permission for the students to have weapons in their dorms. This encouragement is inviting a shootout.

Ranchers in Burns, Oregon, called fellow ranchers to engage in an armed protest and occupied a federal building. This action is not a right to assemble and petition the government under the First Amendment. Rather it is an act of defiance and intimidation, provoking the police to violent action, even though the leader of the protest said they would not fire the first shot. Even that language suggests they were expecting a shootout. This incident was settled without any shooting.

On November 1, 2017, Scott Ostrem walked into a Walmart in suburban Denver and started shooting people with his handgun. He killed two people and a third person died in the hospital. Colorado allows open carry, but local jurisdictions can exempt themselves from that law. Denver does not allow assault rifles or open carry in its limits. [71] Stories like these will become even more common, the more guns become available.

Police Shootings

In 2015 police fatally shot 984 people. Of these 41 were women, 257 were black, and 167 Hispanic. 248 had signs of mental illness. [72]

Twelve-year old Tamir Rice was shot and killed by Officer Timothy Loman on November 22, 2014 in Cleveland, Ohio. Dispatch notified Loman and his partner of an active shooter and proceeded accordingly. They were not notified that the person may have been a child. Tamir weighed 175 pounds so he looked like an adult. When he reached into his belt for his toy gun, Loman shot and killed him. The video tape showed Loman was acting responsibly according to the grand jury and was not charge with a crime.

About the same time as Rice's shooting, protesters gathered in Ferguson, Missouri and New York to protest the deaths of Michael Brown and Eric Garner in those cities. [73]

In October 2014 police video showed that Officer Jason VanDyke shot 17-year-old Laquan McDonald in Chicago 16 times, the majority of shots fired as the teenager recoiled on the street, helpless. VanDyke was charged with first degree murder and arraigned but was released on bond, unusual in first degree murder charges. [74] He was on trial in January 2018.

On December 26, 2015 Chicago police shot and killed 19-year old Quintonio LeGrier, who was allegedly wielding a baseball bat, along with a bystander, Bettie Jones. Chicago police issued an apology, saying Jones was shot accidentally. The shootings occurred outside a Burger King which also had surveillance tape but 82 minutes of the video has been deleted. Another video shows a police officer tampering with a tape at Burger King. [75]

On July 17, 2015 Memphis police officer Connor Schilling shot and killed 19-year old Darrius Stewart after he was stopped for a traffic violation. Schilling was not indicted, but the United States Department of Justice was investigating the case. [76]

Very few police shootings result in convictions of police officers. Of the thousands of shootings since 2005, only 54 officers have been charged with fatally shooting someone while on duty. 35 cases have been resolved with only 11 convictions.

"Prosecutors are often reluctant to pursue these cases, for many reasons: They have long-standing relationships with the police and may hesitate when officers are involved in a fatal shooting, and they also worry they will make police reluctant to put themselves in harm's way, out of fear of making an error, said Randolph McLaughlin, a professor at Pace Law School in White Plains, N.Y., and a civil rights lawyer who works with police shooting cases."

"Juries tend to find police eyewitnesses more credible than average citizens. They also are easily persuaded that excessive force, while distasteful, is often necessary. Judges also tend to favor the police in shooting cases, criminal-law experts say." [77]

Mass Shootings

Mass shootings are especially horrific forms of death by firearms because they impress on our imagination the slaughter that just occurred at a school, church, post office, business, or military base. They have become more common in recent years but the deaths from mass shootings comprise a very small percentage of the total deaths by firearms. Because of their horrific image, they constitute a problem which requires special attention.

Generally, a mass shooting is any incident in which four or more people, not counting the shooter, are killed by gunshot, according to the Gun Violence Archive. [78] There were 146 mass shootings between 1967 and 2017 with an average of eight people dead in each including the perpetrator. The United States experiences more mass shootings than any other country. Eleven of the worst 50 occurred in the United States. The rate of mass shootings has increased significantly since 2011 with one occurring about every two months. [79]

On June 12, 2016 a 29-year-old man, armed with an automatic rifle and a handgun, entered a gay night club in Orlando, Florida and killed 49 people, injuring dozens more. There was an armed guard on duty, but he was helpless in this situation.

A 64-year-old Mesquite, Nevada resident carried 23 firearms and a supply of ammunition in ten pieces of luggage to his room on the 32nd floor at the Mandalay Bay Resort and Casino in Las Vegas in preparation for shooting people who were attending the Route 91 Harvest Music Festival, taking place across the street. On October 1, 2017, he killed at least 58 people and wounded 527 more in the deadliest shooting in modern U.S. history. The 23 firearms included rifles, some with a scope, and handguns. Twelve of them were modified to mimic automatic rifles. Police also found ammonium nitrate, a substance used in explosives, in his car. [80]

Just a month later, on November 5, 2017, a 26-year-old man, using a semi-automatic rifle, killed 26 people at the First Baptist Church in Sutherland Springs, Texas.[81]

Solution

After the mass shooting at Sandy Hook Elementary School in Newtown, Connecticut, the National Rifle Association (NRA) on December 21, 2012 proposed several contributing factors to such massacres including violent video games, media demonization of gun owners, lack of school security and "genuine monsters" planning other attacks. Wayne LaPierre, executive Vice President of the NRA said the solution is armed security in every school which he wanted done by the time children returned from their holiday break. LaPierre said that because politicians pass laws declaring schools gun free zones "they tell every insane killer in America that schools are their safest place to inflict maximum mayhem with minimum risk." He then asked, "How have our nation's priorities gotten so far out of order?"

To bolster his argument, LaPierre reminded us that we have armed security for the president, Congress, banks, courts, and airports. Why not schools? Retired policemen would flock to fill these positions, he suggested. However, LaPierre's examples of armed security involve protecting people or material that others want to destroy or steal for purposes of greed, anger, or power. Schools are a different situation entirely.

LaPierre then suggested that the country is filled with "deranged" people just waiting for the opportunity to repeat what the shooter did in Newtown. He suggested "an active national database of the mentally ill" be established. This is a totally unacceptable proposal for several reasons. First of all, this assumes that all killers are mentally ill or that all mentally ill people are potential killers. While there may be comfort in thinking that way, this idea is not based on reality. Also, who determines whether a person is "mentally ill"? Is the definition "those who have sought help"? To put them on a registry would violate the confidentiality of the professional-patient relationship. If a person is mentally ill, the possibility of being listed on a registry would deter them from seeking help. Lastly, many individuals who struggle with mental illness do not seek help or cannot access it and therefore are not known.

LaPierre declared that the NRA is willing to work with others in developing "a model national schools shield emergency response program" that extends "from armed security to building design and access control, to information technology, to student and teacher training."

Unfortunately, LaPierre did not address the fact that guns are readily available, from both illegal and legal sources, and access to guns must also be considered in searching for solutions to gun violence. The NRA must also be prepared to consider restrictions on the purchase of some types of guns or legal or illegal modifications of guns. In fact he took a contrary point of view by saying that the 20,000 laws already on the books did not prevent this tragedy. He went on to say that "The only thing that stops a bad guy with a gun is a good guy with a gun." In other words, his answer to this mass shooting is more guns!

After the shooting in Orlando, Donald Trump, presumptive Republican presidential nominee at the time, said that if people at the club had guns strapped to their ankles or in their coats, they could have shot the killer . The NRA objected because even the NRA does not want to mix alcohol and guns.

Many gun owners oppose any kind of restrictions on the ownership of guns, being goaded by fear that these restrictions are the beginning of a total ban. This fear, of course, is fueled by the NRA and the powerful gun lobby. Others are open to restrictions, especially background checks and a greater vigilance on keeping people with mental illness from getting their hands on a gun. After the Orlando massacre in 2016, it was proposed that people who are suspected terrorists and are on a "no-fly" list should be prevented from buying a firearm. It was also proposed to institute universal background checks. Republicans in the Senate and House refused to support these bills.

Background checks will work only if people are reported to a national data base. In many cases this is not being done so when a seller checks the background, the buyer is not on the list.

Greater safety instruction in the use and care of firearms must be initiated. A firearm should never be accessible by a child.

Part of the reason the 20,000 laws about guns do not achieve their goal is lack of enforcement. Nancy Kaffer, a columnist for the Detroit *Free Press*, pointed out that the U.S. Bureau of Alcohol, Tobacco, Firearms and Explosives (ATF), which "is the federal agency charged with ensuring that the American gun trade complies with federal and state laws, and with tracking down illegal gun activity," is woefully underfunded and understaffed, primarily due to some members of Congress who keep it that way.

There are 139,000 gun shops in the United States. The ATF has so few inspectors that these shops do not receive a visit from the ATF for as long as eight years. Increasing funding and staffing would allow the ATF to monitor the sale of firearms more effectively. This step could be taken without changing any law or violating the Second Amendment. [82]

The gun industry must be held accountable for many of the deaths caused by guns, especially in mass shootings where automatic and military style weapons are used. Politicians are afraid to confront the gun industry partly because the industry contributes to their election campaigns. As an example, "the gun lobby spent more than $30 million supporting Trump, more money than any other outside group and more than double what it spent to support Mitt Romney in 2012."[83] The law to grant immunity to gun manufacturers for any liability for deaths from their weapons must be repealed. The National Rifle Association (NRA) must be confronted by leaders and voters.

After the shooting at the Marjory Stoneman Douglas High School on February 14, 2018, students decided it was time to act since the adults were not doing anything to stop the violence. They began protest marches, school walkouts, and met with their legislators to demand change. Businesses heard the students' pleas and began to take action. On February 28, 2018 Dick's Sporting Goods and its 35 subsidiary Field & Stream stores announced that they will no longer sell assault rifles

Walmart said it will require buyers of guns and ammunition to be at least age 21. The company stopped selling semi-automatic rifles in 2015 and does not sell bump stocks or high-capacity magazines. MetLife Insurance, First National Bank of Omaha, Symantec, Hertz and Delta Air Lines ended discounts offered to members of the National Rifle Association (NRA).

The NRA in its typical knee-jerk reaction said, "The loss of a discount will neither scare nor distract one single NRA member from our mission to stand and defend the individual freedoms that have always made America the greatest nation in the world." [84]

It is time to end the ideology and focus on solutions to the gun violence in our country, because victims of gun violence also have the right to life, liberty, and the pursuit of happiness.

Prisoners

Prisoners and convicts are people, too, and must be treated with respect and decency. Their punishment must fit the crime and provide an opportunity for the convict to enter society upon release from incarceration. Unfortunately, our country fails in many ways regarding those we imprison.

The world population as of December 2017 was about 7.6 billion, according to UN estimates. The US had a population of 323.1 million or 4.24% of the world population. In 2017 there were more than 2.3 million people incarcerated in the United States in the various federal and state prisons, local jails, and other places of confinement. A half million of those in federal prisons are there on drug-related charges. In addition there are 840,000 people on parole and 3.7 million people on probation.   This makes for a total of 7.8 million people in our correctional system. [85] This means we have an incarceration rate of 991 per 100,000 population, far higher than any other country in the world. Russia's rate is about half and other countries are even lower. We have 4.4% of the world population but 26% of the world's prisoners. The state rates of imprisonment vary greatly from Maine at one-fifth the national rate to Louisiana at double the national rate. [86]

Who Is in Prison?

According to the Federal Bureau of Prisons, 77.6% of federal inmates are U.S. citizens (as of April 2016). 15.2% are citizens of Mexico, and most of the others are from Central America. The Bureau did not state how many had come to the U.S. legally. [87]

"The Vera Institute of Justice reported in 2015 that jails throughout the United States have become warehouses for the poor, the mentally ill and those suffering from addiction as such individuals lack the financial means or mental capacity to post bail."[88]

21% of the people in state prisons were there for drug-related offenses, whereas the percentage in federal prisons was over 60%, according to the Bureau of Prisons statistics.[89]

The number of women in prison has grown from a little over 11,000 in 1977 to more than 213,000 in 2013. Women are caught in ever increasing numbers because of a provision in the law which allows the police to seek partners, relatives and bystanders.

Why?

President Richard Nixon pursued a policy of a war on drugs and was able to get passed the Comprehensive Drug Abuse Prevention and Control Act of 1970. President Ronald Reagan continued the war on drugs with the passage of the Anti-Drug Abuse Act of 1986. Since then, "the United States penal population rose from around 300,000 to more than two million", an increase of over 650%. Incarceration for non-violent offenses dramatically increased, primarily because "the Act imposed the same five-year mandatory sentence on those with convictions involving crack as on those possessing 100 times as much powder cocaine" and "this had a disproportionate effect on low-level street dealers and users of crack, who were more commonly poor blacks, Latinos, the young, and women." About half the people in state prisons and a whopping 90% of those in federal prisons are there for non-violent crimes. [90]

With bipartisan support, the Fair Sentencing Act of 2010 was enacted into law. It reduced "the disparity between the amount of crack cocaine and powder cocaine needed to trigger certain federal criminal penalties from a 100:1 weight ratio to an 18:1 weight ratio and eliminated the five-year mandatory minimum sentence for simple possession of crack cocaine." [91] Some courts had acted in advance of this legislation to reduce the disparity.

Clearly, "drug crimes have been the predominant reason for new admissions into state and federal prisons in recent decades" and rolling back the war on drugs would solve part of the problem, according to the Brookings Institute. [92]

Longer prison sentences and increases in the likelihood of imprisonment are two more factors contributing to the rising incarceration rate in the United States over the past forty years, according to the National Research Council. For example, "the average burglary sentence in the United States is 16 months, compared to 5 months in Canada and 7 months in England." Many states have passed "three-strikes laws", which require a mandatory sentence of 25 years in many cases. [93]

63 percent to 66 percent of those involved in crimes are under the age of thirty. People incarcerated at a younger age lose the capability to invest in themselves and in their communities. Their children and families become susceptible to financial burdens preventing them from escaping low-income communities. This contributes to the recurring cycle of poverty that is positively correlated with incarceration. Poverty rates have not been curbed despite steady economic growth. Poverty is not the sole dependent variable for increasing incarceration rates. Incarceration leads to more incarceration by putting families and communities at a dynamic social disadvantage. [94]

This high incarceration rate is also a racist and political issue. The disparity of punishment between crack and powder cocaine was a direct racist act because it was known to affect minorities and poor people more widely. Not only has this act jailed people but their imprisonment has disrupted family life. Yet we blame them for having poor family values and life.

It is a political issue as well because citizens convicted of a felony cannot vote. As a result, a million or more people are barred from voting who would generally vote Democratic. The act written to be tough on crime was also tough on blacks and their families. It was designed to give Republicans more leverage in who gets elected.

Cost of Correctional System

"State and local spending on incarceration has grown three times as much as spending on public education since 1980", according to a 2016 analysis of federal data by the U.S. Education Department. [95]

The cost for corrections (which includes prisons, jails, probation, and parole) was around $74 billion in 2007, according to The U.S. Bureau of Justice Statistics [96] and is estimated to be around $80 billion now.

Inmates and their families also pay a price for incarceration. These fees include fines and fees for arrest, booking, pre-trial court costs, trial court costs, and other fees attached to the system. In addition there can be attorney fees. The result for a released prisoner s a person in debt. This is especially burdensome because so many prisoners are poor. [97]

Carrie Pettus-Davis, director of the Concordance Institute for Advancing Social Justice and co-director of the Smart Decarceration

Initiative, said the cost of $80 billion per year does not take into account the social costs. Doctoral student Michael McLaughlin,with the assistance of Pettus-Davis, led a study in 2016, which concluded that the costs are $1.2 trillion, 6% of gross domestic product (GDP), per year when the costs to incarcerated persons, families, children and communities are included. The title of the study is The Economic Burden of Incarceration in the U.S.[98]

Crime Rates

Incarceration has increased as much as 500% in the last forty years, yet, property and violent crime rates dropped 30% annually between 1991 and 2001 and another 22% annually between 2001 and 2012. [99]The reason for falling crime rates cannot be ascribed to mass incarceration, according to the Brennan Center for Justice. [100]

Gallup polling since 1989 has found that in most years in which there was a decline in the U.S. crime rate, a majority of Americans said that violent crime was getting worse. [101]

In a preliminary study by the Brennan Center for Justice, the crime rate for 2017 is projected to be down to the lowest point since 1991. There is no current crime wave. [102]

Prison Privatization

The Republicans have been the prime movers in the "tough on crime" policy resulting in massive prison building. Then, in an effort to save money, the Republicans sought to and succeeded in allowing private corporations to operate prisons. Prior to the 1980's there were no private prisons. Instead of saving money however, these actions have had two disastrous effects. Private companies have sought and obtained contracts which guarantee 90% occupancy thus forcing the courts to send more people to prison. Otherwise, the state will be paying for empty cells. The public goal was to have a more efficient system and to save money, but privatization has done neither.

The second disastrous effect is that these for-profit prison companies also belong to the organization American Legislative Exchange Council (ALEC), which writes proposed laws to submit to the legislatures. Their proposed laws, however, have a self-interest rather than the interest of the prisoners.

Louisiana, for example, has the highest rate of incarceration in the world with the majority of its prisoners being housed in privatized, for-profit facilities. Such institutions could face bankruptcy without a steady influx of prisoners. A 2013 Bloomberg report states that in the past decade the number of inmates in for-profit prisons throughout the U.S. rose 44 percent. [103]

Private prison companies have billions of dollars in annual revenue not only from the tax dollars but from the sale of goods produced by free labor, thus competing unfairly with private enterprise. These prisons cost about

$30,000 per year per inmate. This scheme actually produces more prisoners than fewer because the for-profit companies need the inmates in order to stay in business.

Life in Prison

There are many other factors that must be considered that are results of incarceration. There need to be federal and state prison programs offering education, retraining for jobs, and instruction on how to live within the law.

Matthew De Michael (Ph.D. from William Penn University) notes that "money is not invested in reform programs to help get prisoners out of jail and off with jobs." A felon's chances of getting a job are reduced by 78%, some say. As a result, they all too often resort to what they know: drug dealing and other criminal activity. So they end up back in jail. In most cases felons are also denied the right to vote. [104]

It is important to note that people in prison do not lose their basic human rights and these must not be violated. While they have lost the right of free movement by being incarcerated, imprisonment does not mean they lose the right to health care, physical activity, protection from abuse, and the right to read and enjoy life in their limited space. The incarceration is the punishment, not the denial of basic human rights, according to Penal Reform International.

Reform

The Brennan Center for Justice for all "seeks to secure our nation's promise of "equal justice for all" by creating a rational, effective, and fair justice system. Its priority focus is to <u>reduce mass incarceration</u> while keeping down crime. The program melds law, policy, and economics to produce new empirical analyses and innovative policy solutions to advance this critical goal." [105]

Sen. Chuck Grassley (R-IA) had a bill, the Sentencing Reform and Corrections Act, pass out of his committee in 2016 with strong bipartisan support. The proposal was also backed by law enforcement people, judges, and others. The bill died in Congress,

Both House Speaker Paul Ryan (R-WI) and Grassley were committed to introducing sentence reform legislation in 2017 and agreed that such legislation was long overdue, but there has been no action.

Attorney General Jeff Sessions issued a directive that reinstated outdated federal charging policies which had led to mass incarceration. In contrast, the Brennan Center for Justice at NYU School of Law in May 2017 presented "four pieces of legislation and three executive actions" to reform the criminal justice system.

The plan, which I support, suggests legislation to:

End the Federal Subsidization of Mass Incarceration and use that money as incentives to states to reduce crime and incarceration in their state.

End Federal Incarceration for Lower-Level Crimes: This savings would more than pay for the incentives.

Institute a Police Corps Program to Modernize Law Enforcement: To advance a twenty-first century police force, Congress can create a program to recruit and train new officers in modern policing tactics focused on crime prevention, reducing unnecessary arrests and use of force, and increasing community engagement.

Enact Sentencing Reform: Congress can reintroduce and pass the Sentencing Reform and Corrections Act of 2015.

The three executive actions the Center recommends are:

Redirect Federal Grants Away from Mass Incarceration

Institute New Goals for Federal Prosecutors

Commute Sentences to Retroactively Apply the Fair Sentencing Act of 2010: [106]

Incarceration does not rehabilitate prisoners and many are worse off upon release than before incarceration. We need rehabilitation programs.

The Elderly

We have a most unusual way of dealing with the elderly in our country. Societies for millennia have revered the elderly for their wisdom gained from experience and have put them in positions of responsibility. There is much talent among the elderly that is not being tapped to make life better for everyone. The individualism so revered in this country continues into old age, so that elderly people are frequently shuffled off into retirement homes where all too often there are inadequate services.

The elderly deserve a comfortable old age with proper food, suitable clothing, a warm home, access to health care, and the ability to go from place to place in the community. Those who are disabled in some way, and of course many of the elderly are, need to have these needs attended to.

Most importantly, however, we need to respect the wisdom gained by their experience. Many live very active lives after retirement and this way of life must be fully encouraged and utilized.

All Lives Matter

We are challenged to cherish all lives at every stage of growth and development. We need to find candidates for public office who will champion the lives of all people without discrimination. We need candidates who look upon people with compassion, not judgement, and who want to help people move along the journey of life.

5. Everything Is Interconnected

While the issues described in the previous chapters are certainly interrelated with each other and with people in all aspects of their lives, the issues in this chapter are societal in nature. They must be talked about in relationships of various kinds because they all impact each other significantly.

Economy

The economy is not all about business but also involves how we manufacture products or provide services. The economy not only requires capital but also employees who must be educated to perform their jobs, be healthy and be able to get to their jobs. Let's take a look at capitalism, our preferred business model.

Capitalism

Capitalism is a great economic system, especially if you are one who has benefited by it. Many people have a reverence for it that is almost religious. Unfortunately, this reverence is similar to the reverence that used to be given to the Bible by those who put it in a safe place in the house, not to be touched or read.

What Adam Smith described in the *Wealth of Nations* in 1776 is a free market that mostly consisted of many small entrepreneurs providing a product or service. Often the family was integral to the operation of this business. In this system workers were respected for the talents they had because capitalism was undergirded by high moral principles and values. Excessive profits were a detriment to the smooth operation of capitalism according to Smith. Shortly after Smith published his book, the Industrial Revolution exploded. More and more small businesses were replaced with larger ones until today the vestiges of the small family entrepreneurial operation hardly exist. Even though most of the jobs in this country are provided by small enterprises, our economic system is dominated and controlled by the large multinational corporations that do not even resemble the capitalism Smith described in his book.

The Industrial Revolution changed the whole manner of competition, employment, and ownership. In 1886 the U.S. Supreme Court ruled that a corporation was a legal person, using the 14th Amendment as its basis for such an argument.

> *In 1886, . . . in the case of Santa Clara County v. Southern Pacific Railroad Company, the U.S. Supreme Court decided that a private*

The corporation had existed for many years but this decision allowed wealthy people to engage in business ownership with limited liability and risk to their own wealth. In the process corporations became very entwined with government and capitalism, as envisioned by Smith, never came to exist.

In 2010 the Supreme Court decided in the *Citizens United* case that corporations have the right of free speech that is guaranteed under the First

Amendment. [108] From this decision have come Super PACS which receive and dole out billions of dollars for the purpose of influencing political races under the guise of education. This decision in *Citizens United* has created many problems and the decision must be overturned.

Employees

Capitalism derives its name from the capital (wealth) which owners use to start and maintain a business operation. Employees are an integral part of any business unless of course the business is a one-person operation. Employees are people, not a resource like steel, oil or inventory. In fact, as George Lakoff wrote in his book, *The All New Don't Think of an Elephant*, , "workers are profit creators." They need to be treated with respect and dignity. Employees take a risk when they choose to work for a particular company, expecting to receive the rewards of decent wages, benefits, and security in exchange for their work and commitment to the company. This part of capitalism is sadly overlooked or ignored in our economic discussions and is the reason for the emergence of labor unions.

To dramatize the risks an employee takes when accepting a job, consider the following fictional letter from an employee to an employer:

Dear Business Owner/Employer:

It is a good thing that you have taken the risk of starting or running a business, since that is where jobs come from for people like me. Because you provide the capital, it is assumed that you are taking all the risk in this endeavor. We even call our economic system "capitalism" after this aspect of it and workers (labor) are often referred to as "human resources".

You aren't the only one taking a risk, however. I have taken a risk in accepting a job in your company. I am investing the most important assets I have: my time and skills. I am risking these assets in your company. For example:

When I asked for a higher salary, you told me to get a job somewhere else that pays higher. But I love what I do, I said, and stayed working for you.

When I urged my fellow employees to set up a union, you fired me. All I wanted was an opportunity to share in the decisions that you make regarding my working conditions.

When I first joined the union, you stopped speaking to me. You figured I was a traitor of some sort, but I just wanted a fair shake by joining together with my fellow employees.

When you passed me over for a job promotion because I am a woman, I felt the sting of being just another tool in your business operation, not a human being.

When I worked as a food server in your restaurant, I cheerfully took orders and served the customers, even though they didn't seem to appreciate it.

When I challenged you about unethical practices, you gave me thirty days' notice. I was out looking for a different job, even though I gave dedicated service to your fledgling operation.

When you reorganized the company and put me in a position that I didn't apply for nor am I fully qualified for, I still carried on. You even gave me a heavier work load and I worked harder.

When I performed my services well, you gave me new responsibilities and a fancy job title, but no increase in compensation or staff to aid me in that new position.

When you read my resume, you were excited to meet with me for an interview, but you gave me a lesser position because you saw the color of my skin.

I worked for your start-up operation without many benefits, because I was willing to take that risk and succeed along with you.

You provided health insurance, a retirement plan, and paid days off for vacation, holidays, and family emergencies. Although these benefits were significant, I still faced the risk of losing them if I was let go or left your employment.

I worked in good faith for many years building up my own 401(k) plan only to have it ripped out from under me because of your unethical business practices.

You had me travel for days and weeks at a time at the expense of being with my family.

When I turned 55, you downsized your business and let me go.

Because you thought of me only as a tool for success, you had me work in unhealthy circumstances. Now I am unable to enjoy my retirement.

I went back to school to increase my skills so I could do my job even better. I paid for this out of my own money even though you benefited from my new knowledge.

You see, I, too, took a risk with my time and skills, my very life, by going to work for you. I ask for the recognition of my contribution not only in your company but towards the healthy status of our economic system. I am not just another resource to be used and then tossed out when you don't need me any more.

Sincerely,
Your faithful employee

Unions

Jim (not his real name) and I had several email exchanges regarding capitalism. He challenged me to come up with a better system than capitalism since I was critical of its operation. Then he wrote about the good life capitalism has brought him after retiring from Dow Chemical. He has enjoyed a good home, vacations, and now "I am pretty much self sufficient and I do enjoy Social Security and Medicare benefits."

I responded, "Capitalism did not provide you the benefits you listed – your employer did that…. the owners of business control what they do, how much they pay themselves, and how much they pay their employees.." His Social Security and Medicare are, of course, from the government, not his employer.

Jim wrote, "the company is bound, through collective bargaining with the union, to perform in an agreed upon system! They cannot arbitrarily fire anyone without cause!"

I replied that he made my case very well that capitalism and the free market do not work for the benefit of employees. Unions are not part of capitalism. They were formed and legally supported by government to force companies to be fair! A better system than capitalism is a combination of capitalism and government involvement. That's what we have. Fine tuning the relationship is always necessary.

Jim is a person who has railed against candidate and then President Obama while touting the benefits of Social Security and Medicare as if they were products of his own work and not government programs. He wrote he was a "self sufficient man" without recognizing the benefits guaranteed through his labor union. None of these sources of his security and self sufficiency that he praises are aspects of capitalism but rather come from government regulation of capitalism. It is important to understand our economic system if we are to move forward without being hampered by ignorance.

Technological Revolution

Our world is in a post-industrial age. Industry is no longer the driving force in the economies of the wealthy nations but rather technology drives the economy. While technology has created wonderful tools and toys, especially in the areas of medicine, chemical industries, and communication, the disruption it causes by rapid change is difficult to bear. Thomas Friedman wrote in *Thank You for Being Late* that it takes human beings 15 years to adapt to a change in the way we live and think. Changes, however, are taking place every six years. These changes are causing many physical and mental challenges. Advances in technology have created power in the hands of those who possess this knowledge, unprecedented in the history of our world.

Pope Francis addressed the issue in his letter on the environment, *Laudato Si*, in which he wrote that people have "'not been trained to use power well', [109] because our immense technological development has not been accompanied by a development in human responsibility, values and conscience.'"" [110]

Futuristic cityscape/technology concept

Technology and the power it creates become ends in themselves instead of valuing them in the context of our culture and society. People in charge of technology fail to look at the bigger picture because they are too enraptured by their own technological searching and developments.

Socialism

During Obama's campaign for the presidency, opponents and pundits raised the question of socialism. According to the Merriam-Webster dictionary, socialism is "any of various social systems based on shared or government ownership and administration of the means of production and distribution of goods". When Obama told Joe the Plumber during the 2008 campaign that he wanted to "spread the wealth around", there was an immediate attack on Obama for uttering these words.

Barbara West, a reporter in Florida, asked vice-presidential candidate Joe Biden, "You may recognize this famous quote, 'from each according to his abilities, to each according to his needs.' That's from Karl Marx. How is Sen. Obama not being a Marxist if he intends to spread the wealth around?" Biden was taken aback and expressed his surprise in the question by asking

West, "Are you joking? Is this a joke? ... Or is that a real question?" [111] Then Biden went on to answer the question in the negative. Instead of dealing with the issue of "spreading the wealth around", West chose rather to engage in the fear of socialism. The reality of the past 36 years, however, is that there has been an enormous redistribution of wealth from the lower and middle classes to the top 1% of the population.

Billy Wharton, editor of the Socialist magazine, analyzed Obama's policies from a Socialist Party position and emphatically stated that Obama is no Socialist. He also added that all the talk by Mike Huckabee, Rush Limbaugh and others about socialism is bringing new members to the Socialist Party in numbers he hasn't seen in decades. [112] Could these rising numbers also support Sen. Bernie Sanders' strong bid for the Democratic presidential nomination in 2016?

Is Marxism (socialism) the only form of spreading the wealth around? President Ronald Reagan in 1980 ushered in a new era of conservative Republicanism. The income gap between the CEOs and the lowest paid employees was 40 to 1 then. The gap has now ballooned nearly eleven times that to 433 to 1 according to *Forbes* [113] . Now that gap illustrates "spreading the wealth from the lower and middle-income people to the wealthiest". This redistribution has created much more poverty in the U.S.

The rise in this income gap was not an accident. It was orchestrated by lower taxes on the wealthy and considerable deregulation of the business sector. The same policies existed in the 1920's, a period of "very unhealthy corporate and banking structures, an unsound foreign trade, much economic misinformation" and a large gap in income. [114] Sound familiar? Those policies led to the stock market crash in 1929 and the Great Depression which continued for more than a decade. Those words could just as well have been used to describe the years leading to the meltdown of the stock market in September 2008 and subsequent bailout of the financial industry.

The Great Depression and the market meltdown in 2008 show the weakness of capitalism which is based on profit motivation. Capitalism as a theory has nothing to do with morals and ethics, but since human beings act within this system, all the weaknesses of human morality, like greed, manipulation and fraud, get injected into capitalism and thus large income gaps, recessions, and depressions occur. Capitalism has nothing to do with the common good, which is an essential consideration if we are going to have a thriving society, not just a thriving economy. Today our government and corporate leaders, as well as the voters in both political parties, fail to look at the common good.

Socialism is based on a theory of common ownership of property and the means of production. Social programs aim to minimize the weaknesses of our capitalistic economy. Social Security is a social program that has proven to be a lifesaver for millions of people. Obama's plans for taxes, health care, and energy were not socialism but programs based on social justice.

In addition, the government has been doling out financial benefits to business from the very beginning. There have been and are tariffs, for example, to protect American business from foreign competition. We have been supporting farming for many years with subsidies. Airlines have benefited from the government dole. The entire oil industry still reaps enormous tax benefits while taking in billions of dollars of profit. The railroads of the nineteenth century were given millions of acres of land along the track right-of-way which they sold for a great deal of profit. The railroads were even paid one million dollars per mile of track laid. While capitalism fails the common good by allowing wealth to accumulate among the top five percent, socialism fails in not compensating hard work enough. Yet capitalism is failing to pay hard working people enough in the 21st century.

One of the signs of socialism, according to opponents of government benefits, is the national debt. This was especially true when trillions of dollars were used for bailouts and economic stimulus in 2009 and 2010. But I find it hypocritical of Republicans to be talking of the danger of deficits when the Republicans are responsible for the growth of the national debt from 1 trillion in 1980 to over 10 trillion in 2008. It grew only 1 trillion under Democrat Bill Clinton (1993-2001).

Unfortunately, the national debt has again doubled during the years of the Obama administration but the reason for it lies squarely in the 535 members of Congress who rail against big deficits but do nothing about them. Now in 2017 with a Republican Congress and Republican President, once again tax cuts were passed that will add to the deficit and national debt by $1.5 trillion, according to some estimates. In February 2018 Congress voted to keep the government in operation and added another trillion to the debt. While the Democrats are not innocent over the years, they are not responsible for the latest tax cuts.

Managing the Economy

Progressive policies and programs are not socialism. Capitalism is not a god to be adored but a system to be used for the general welfare as declared in our Constitution. The only way to make that happen is through managing the economy. Some people object to this language but as I have said many times, there is no such thing as a free market and there never has been. The government has been involved in the economy from the very beginning.

The entire financial sector of our economy is the linchpin of capitalism. If it fails, we all fail. That's why it is so important for this sector of our economy to run smoothly with safeguards and protection for all of us.

Unfortunately, since 1980 under both Republican and Democratic leadership we have seen just the opposite happening.

The Glass-Steagall Act was passed in 1933 to keep banks, insurance companies, and investment companies separate from each other. The act was repealed in 1998 during the Clinton administration and its repeal is believed by some to have been a cause of the 2008 recession, the worst since the Great Depression. For 65 years this act helped to keep the economy running smoothly with minor dips. [115] Clinton did not support the repeal but signed it because Congress had enough votes to override a veto.

As a result of the repeal, banking and securities were allowed to operate without much regard for oversight. Banks were encouraged to offer sub-prime mortgages in order to expand home ownership. Many lenders were imprudent in their practices and so were consumers with the result that many people had mortgages not suitable to their financial situation.

Investment bankers then decided to bundle these mortgages and other debt instruments and sell them to people like you and me. One problem is that they did not know how to evaluate the legality and risk of these investments. This action opened the door to such people as Bernie Madoff who bilked his clients of $50 billion in allegedly fraudulent securities.

According to BBC News, when the whistleblower Harry Markopolos told the Securities and Exchange Commission (SEC) about Bernie Madoff in 2000, the SEC chose not to investigate. [116] When the SEC finally investigated Madoff's scheme in 2006 it could find nothing illegal or unethical. Apparently even the SEC regulators did not understand these investments. Fifty billion dollars, by the way, is the equivalent of $16 million for every Midland, Michigan (where I live) household.

As a result of the crisis in the financial sector, banks closed the door on credit but that did not solve the problem. In fact it had a ripple effect on stable corporations which rely on credit to operate their businesses. It also limited you and me in our buying of cars and other items on credit. Home equity loans dried up to 2% of the number of them in 2006.

Nearly a trillion dollars was injected into the economy during 2008 to stave off the ill effects of a looming recession, but that money did little good. The economy kept getting worse. The first tactic in 2008 was to give rebates to taxpayers (remember that?). Then the government injected money into AIG and other financial firms to offset their lousy management and investing.

In 2009 a stimulus package took effect to jump start jobs in energy, the arts, health care, roads, schools, and other infrastructure – spending that went to working people. Our national parks were falling into disrepair and neglect because of a lack of adequate funding. Money for energy went a long way in providing an impetus towards alternative energy. Social programs, such as food stamps and other welfare benefits including unemployment compensation, enhanced the economy because the recipients spent that money rather than save it.

Tax cuts were also included in the recovery package but tax cuts for the wealthy were part of the reason we were in such a mess in 2009. Tax cuts in 1983, 2001 and 2003 have created the wealthiest class since the 1920's. The top 1% of earners in the U.S. take home 20% of the national income. After the tax cuts of 2017, they will be enjoying even more wealth.

Proper tax increases can actually boost the economy. Even President Reagan realized this. After his huge tax reduction in 1981 there came the largest tax increase in 1986 since World War II. Trickle-down economics has been proven a failure and it is time to move on. There is too much political partisan posturing on both sides.Tax increases in 1993 boosted the economy and produced a balanced budget under President Clinton.

During President Obama's two terms, much progress was made toward economic recovery. December 2016 marked 79 months of steady job growth under President Obama. This growth is the longest growth period since the Great Depression. This growth continued during President Trump's first year in office for which he tries to take credit, but the fall of the market in February 2018 tells a different story about the Trump administration.

The economy is a fundamental aspect of the entire American fabric as it links employment to families' well being. When the economy is strong, people are working and healthier, people can go on vacation and enjoy events outside the home, and plan for the future. They can pay for education and plan for retirement. Everyone buys not only the essentials but other items to use.

Health care

Health care reform in various formats has been on the national agenda ever since World War II. A major reform took place when the Affordable Care Act was passed in 2010, despite the distortion, fear and outright lies offered by opponents.

Two issues involving health care are seldom ever clarified. There is the concern for access to health care and there is concern about who pays for it. The latter is generally the role of health insurance. Access to good health care is dependent on having health insurance or a lot of wealth and health care providers nearby.

Despite the claim in 2009 by Rush Limbaugh that "there's no health-care crisis in this country",[117] the facts speak otherwise. Most importantly of all, we spent in 2009 more on health care than any other industrialized nation on earth. This is not an insignificant amount but rather twice and three times as much as other countries. Most countries are spending less than one tenth

80

of their income for health care. We spend one of every six dollars on health care, soon to be one of every five,[118] [6] according to David Cay Johnston, an American investigative journalist specializing in economics and tax issues.

A second failure of our health system relates to life expectancy and infant mortality. Why is our life expectancy lower than in 17 other countries? Why is infant mortality greater in the U.S. than in countries like Cuba and Russia? [119]

Opponents of health care reform say that their health care will be rationed under reform. Health care was rationed all the time under our system prior to the Affordable Care Act. Those without insurance or the ability to pay for health care were limited in their access. Those with health insurance were limited by the choice of doctors and clinics, or by exclusion of coverage under the policy for various reasons including pre-existing conditions. One of the most critical areas of rationing was the lack of portability of one's insurance coverage. Health insurance is too often connected with a place of employment. If someone becomes unemployed, there goes the health insurance coverage. Many of these problems were resolved or lessened under the Affordable Care Act.

Waiting for service is also a form of rationing. This issue has not been adequately resolved under reform. We have heard horror stories about long waits in the Canadian and British systems but they have been exceptions rather than the rule for their health care. Under our current system we have long waits for service too. I personally was referred to a clinic in Ann Arbor and the earliest appointment I could get was two months away.

Critics would do well to avoid comparisons to the Canadian or British systems since the Affordable Health Care Act deso not even suggest that type of plan. The critics only add confusion to an already confusing issue.

There are excellent examples of health care that we would do well to adopt. The Mayo Clinic operates in Minnesota, Arizona, and Florida. The Cleveland Clinic is in Cleveland Ohio. Both focus on the patient rather than fee for service model. They run efficiently and are recognized as superior providers of health care. France is also said to have an excellent health care system.

In the 1980's Congress allowed non-profit health insurance organizations to become profit-based companies with the argument that costs would be lower. The reality is that the insurance premiums under these new companies skyrocketed. Greed coupled with blatant refusal to honor claims

---

[6] See also David Cay Johnston, Perfectly Legal: The Covert Campaign to Rig Our Tax System to Benefit the Super-Rich -- and Cheat Everyone Else, New York: Penguin Books, 2003.

made these companies look good in the financial world. They joined the ranks of other corporations with highly compensated executives. In some cases fraud was rampant. [120]

Dr. William Frist, the former Tennessee senator and one-time presidential hopeful, and Richard L. Scott were two people who participated in such private companies. Both were very vocal opponents of current health care reform. Scott's company was convicted of fraud and paid nearly one billion dollars in damages. Scott was ousted from the company and three employees sent to prison.[121] Oversight of Medicare payments would help to stop this kind of fraud and the money saved through oversight would more than offset its cost.

We also have the problem of millions of uninsured people who nevertheless seek health care in emergency situations. These patients cost the rest of us more than it would cost to have these people insured. Insurance would also help uninsured people to seek health care before their situation becomes an emergency.

The Affordable Care Act got off to a bumpy start and struggled at other times but it has provided insurance and health care to more than 18 million people as of February 2016. Republicans have tried to repeal the act over sixty times. In 2017 the Republican controlled Congress tried to repeal the Affordable Care Act several times and replace it with a plan that would deprive millions of health care coverage.   Various parties have taken it to the Supreme Court where it has been upheld twice.

It is important to look at the big picture and the general welfare when thinking about health insurance and access to health care. While the Affordable Care Act did not resolve all the problems, it went a long way in alleviating many of them. Among them were the elimination of the pre-existing clause and the problem of portability. The inclusion of contraceptives created a firestorm of protests, especially by Catholic bishops. We need to fine tune that act rather than repeal it as Republicans want to do. The Republicans did succeed in ending the individual mandate in the act, but this will drive up health insurance costs because fewer people are paying into it.

The real solution to the health care crisis, however, is universal health care coverage, or as some people are calling it, Medicare for all. This plan would accomplish several very important things. First and foremost, everyone would be covered, regardless of their personal financial situation. This universal plan would also include prescriptions. Insurance companies could still be involved for management or additional coverage above what is covered under the plan. Coverage would no longer be dependent on an employer or employment relieving businesses of millions of dollars of expenses involved in the administration of health care plans. This would give the employers greater competitiveness in the market place. Universal health care should lower the costs of products and services and could be paid for through a value added tax (VAT).

The repeal of the individual mandate in the Affordable Care Act led insurance companies to increase their premiums by as much as twenty percent. A projection of the results of the repeal says that many rural hospitals and clinics will go out of existence because they will be receiving much less income resulting in loss of access for millions.

Drugs

Why are drugs so costly?

Lobbyists are people employed to promote their company's products or services. in 2017 the pharmaceutical and health products industry spent $277,784,999 and had 1,480 Lobbyists. [122] The lobbyists direct their attention to members of Congress as well as people in state legislatures to influence favorable laws. They also lobby the Food and drug Administration (FDA), who must alpprove drugs and health products before they can be sold.   Lobbyists also oppose price controls and support patent rights.

In 1997 the Food and Drug Administration allowed companies to advertise their drugs directly to consumers. There is no screening of these ads by the FDA or any other group. Many of these ads direct us to "ask your doctor if this drug is right for you" and thus increase the demand for them. Advertising has paid off for the companies, as sales for advertised products provide as much as half the profit of a company.

CBS News reported that in 2017 the pharmaceutical industry spent $5.2 billion on direct advertising to consumers, up 60% from four years ago.In November 2017, the American Medical Association called for a ban on pharmaceutical ads because doctors believe "the surge in drug ads is prompting consumers to demand expensive medications they might not need".. [123]

Drugs are a vital part of one's personal health. The cost of them must not be left to the vagaries of the marketplace. Pharmaceutical companies must not be allowed to charge any rate they wish for drugs. When prescription drugs are out of reach of someone in need, then the temptation is to resort to illegal drugs.

A direct result of the problem with prescription drugs is the opioid epidemic that is suddenly being recognized for the health problem it is. 60,000 people died in 2016 from the use of these drugs. President Trump did declare the use of these drugs a national emergency but health care professionals said this was not enough. Many of the opioids are obtained by prescription.

Each person needs to be more responsible for his/her own health by healthy behavior and activity, depending on a doctor for situations beyond a person's ability. Good health is of course related to the ability to work and enjoy life.

Environment

Our planet seems to be getting smaller and smaller with all the ways we can travel and communicate with each other. Our human population continues to grow to the point that there are very few places in the world where a group of people are so isolated from others that they have a disconnected way of life.

Most people by contrast do live within a heavily inhabited area so that scarcely a moment goes by that one does not interact with others. This overpopulation, some people would say, is causing a great deal of stress on our world and human interaction. Others, including Pope Francis, say that overpopulation is not the problem but rather our collective unwillingness to set up systems that provide the necessary means for life to grow.

Regardless of how one views the population situation, it is undeniable that all people are very closely interconnected. I tried to show that above in my segment on the economy. But it is much bigger than the economy. It involves all issues of life.

This interconnectedness is not merely among human beings but with all of the plants and animals. All have a place on this earth and must be respected and even cherished because, if for no other reason, they provide the sustenance and other benefits we need for our human lives. . Plants and animals must not be used solely for profit or pleasure. [7]

It is arrogant to think we can use the elements of our world in any way we wish. Their use has repurcussions which are not often assessed. Such is the use of petroleum products. We have polluted the air, water, and land by the use of these and other products. It is believed that there are many more cases of respiratory diseases because of this pollution. Environmental pollution affects health care. Fracking in Oklahoma is believed to be the cause of a substantial increase in the number of earthquakes in that state. Increased use of fertilizers and pesticides has resulted in greater food supplies but at the cost of increased pollution of our environment.

We must change our attitude and practices regarding our world if we are going to save it from total degradation. Our irresponsible use of our world's resources has been partially caused by a misunderstanding of God's command in the book of Genesis to "subdue the earth". Rather that phrase should be translated as "be good stewards of the earth." We are called to do so in a collective manner, as no one has an a exclusive right to own property. The earth is essentially a shared inheritance, whose fruits are meant to benefit everyone, especially the poor and the underprivileged. *A good part of our genetic code is shared by many living beings.* [124]

---

[7] Many of my comments in this section are based on *Laudato Si, (On the Care of Our Common Home)*, by Pope Francis.

The Industrial Revolution of the last two hundred years has brought about great change in our society and culture and caused much human anxiety. Our methods of production do not model the natural recycling pattern in our world. As a result we have caused much pollution of the land, air, and water. In addition we have caused global warming. We need to use alternative energy resources, such as wind and solar power.

Access to clean water is a human right but there is already not enough water in some places of the world, due to pollution and waste as well as its over-use in some areas.

The social dimensions of global change, Pope Francis wrote in *Laudato Si*, include the effects of technological innovations on employment, social exclusion, an inequitable distribution and consumption of energy and other services, social breakdown, increased violence and a rise in new forms of social aggression, drug trafficking, growing drug use by young people, and the loss of identity.

There is also the fact that people no longer seem to believe in a happy future. Progress can no longer be related to technological advances and there is a growing sense that the way to a better future lies elsewhere. To this end, Pope Francis wrote, "Let us refuse to resign ourselves to technocratic paradigm and continue to wonder about the purpose and meaning of everything. [125]

We need to have an integral ecology that takes into account not only the physical aspects of our world but the social dimension as well. It must also include the myriad of plant and animal forms and the various ecosystems.

The culture and history of a given area must also be included in an integral ecology. All of this requires the working together of many specialized fields in science, sociology, and religion. An integral ecology is inseparable from the notion of the common good, a central and unifying principle of social ethics. [126] An integral ecology must take into account the future generations who will be inhabiting the earth after us. We need to reflect on our accountability before those who will have to endure the dire consequences. [127]

Candidates for public office must not only be willing to examine these issues but also make positive recommendations for changes. Cooperation with all the countries of the world will be required. There must be an honest discussion of global warming.

Global warming

We know that global warming is a reality, but many people choose to deny the human contribution to that warming. Exxon-Mobil in its own research in the late 1970's and early 1980's clearly showed that fossil fuels would cause an increase in the earth's temperature, yet chose publicly to take every action to deny their own conclusions. [128]Exxon-Mobil retorts that this claim is a distortion of their research and public policy. [129]

In a letter [130] about our world, Pope Francis emphasized that we have a responsibility to take care of each other and everything in the world. Yet we are largely responsible for the environmental degradation that exists all over the world. We, too, have contributed to the global warming. All of our human actions have caused disharmony with adverse effects especially on the poor. We are heading for global suicide, he said on his flight back from Africa in 2016. [131]

Global warning is a subject that must be addressed and not just thrown away as if there is no substance to the claim that there is climate change that needs to be examined and dealt with.

Infrastructure

Infrastructure refers to the fundamental facilities and systems serving a country, city, or area, including the services and facilities necessary for its economy to function. It typically characterises technical structures such as roads, bridges, tunnels, water supply, sewers, electrical grids, telecommunications, and so forth, and can be defined as "the physical components of interrelated systems providing commodities and services essential to enable, sustain, or enhance societal living conditions."[132]

Infrastructure also refers to assets and facilities such as airports, bridges, broadband access, canals, dams, energy services, hazardous waste removal, hospitals, levees, lighthouses, parks, ports, mass transit, public housing, schools, public spaces, railroads, sewage and solid waste disposal, telecommunications, utilities, water supply and wastewater treatment.

There is a tendency in this country to concern oneself only with the present. That is true in our personal lives as well as civic lives. All of the infrastructure components are interconnected and require a great deal of attention and expense to maintain. Neglecting them will be at our peril as a society and as a country.

President Trump, in his state of the union address on January 30, 2018, advocated spending $1.5 trillion to improve our infrastructure. This plan will not only benefit our infrastructure, it will mean jobs. However, the president was very unrealistic in saying that most of it would be paid by the states and private contractors. States don't have the money and the other suggests selling or giving our roads and other public facilities to private companies.

Education

Education has been a very important part of the social and cultural fabric of this nation from the very beginning. One of the first things the early settlers did was to set up schools in their localities. Our first national government under the Articles of Confederation passed the Northwest

Ordinance of 1787 which fostered education in the rapidly growing Northwest Territory, now roughly the Great Lakes States. Michigan required the establishment of schools while it was still a territory and has never wavered from this support. The attendance requirement gradually increased from a mere three-month school year for primary school children to a school year today of at least 180 days (in Michigan) through twelve grades. Now we are at the point where that requirement must again be increased to some years of college or trade school. Many early schools on the east coast were church related but by the mid-nineteenth century a public school system was gaining widespread popularity and support. It is not surprising that this development occurred at that time since this is the same time that the flow of immigrants to this country was at its all-time high. Many religious schools developed at this time so these immigrants could retain some of their cultural and religious identity. Public schools incorporated these immigrants and their families into the American mainstream. The public schools served us well as they included the values of our society and culture.

That emphasis must be brought back to our schools so that all the elements of our society and culture can once again be coordinated into a fabric of equality and opportunity for all. The powerful, unifying force of public education has been weakened by a strong movement to end public schools and an equally strong movement to lower taxes.

U.S. Secretary of Education Betsy DeVos and her husband Dick have been proponents of schools of choice for many years. Charles and David Koch, politically active conservative billionaires, are allied with the DeVos family as well in the effort to weaken public education.

Charter schools are one result of this effort. These are public schools which receive tax dollars and draw students from a local district but operate independently of the local district in which they are located. The law in Michigan for charter schools requires them to provide a special need in the community. Examples of special needs are low income area, students with English as a second language, children with disabilities, and transportation challenges.

The performance of many charter schools is worse than regular public schools. Nationally, about 75% of charter schools perform worse or no better than the local public school, according to The CREDO study at Stanford in 2013. [133]

Charter schools are not being properly supervised and 80% of them are operated by for-profit businesses, a violation of our Michigan Constitution, in my opinion, because in Michigan, private schools are forbidden by the Michigan Constitution from receiving tax dollars. Dick and Betsy DeVos spent millions on a campaign to overturn this Constitutional ban, but 68% of the voters said "no" to a voucher plan in Michigan.

In its simplest form a voucher is the granting of tax dollars to the pupil to be used at a school of his/her choice, including non-public religious or private schools. Vouchers also refer to money donated by businesses for pupils to use at a school of choice. Usually the business receives a tax credit. Some vouchers are a combination of tax dollars and business dollars.

After the defeat of the voucher proposal in Michigan, Betsy DeVos turned her attention to schools of choice and convinced the legislature to pass a law that allows a student to choose a different school in the district other than the neighborhood school. This law also allowed students to go to a different district if that district would accept him or her. While this idea sounds good on paper, it does not really help the poor student who has no transportation to a different school, nor does it help any student in a district where there is not another elementary, middle, or high school.

Parents in many states have the right to teach their children at home in a process called homeschooling. In Michigan there are no standards for the parents or curriculum requirements. Parents are not required to report to the local district or the state that they are homeschooling their children. Parents are not required to keep any records. As a result of these loose laws, there is no definitive data to show whether homeschooling works.

Charter schools, schools of choice, vouchers for non-public schools, and homeschooling all detract from the universal character of a public school system. We must be very watchful so this movement does not take over the public school system and destroy it.

One of the areas of deep concern to me is the lack of the ability to think clearly and discern options for life and for voting. I suppose this has never been fully dealt with in our educational system, but as the world shrinks, it is more important that we become a better educated citizenry. One example of this kind of education is exploring the difference between fact and opinion.

The late Sen. Daniel Patrick Moynihan (D-NY) said, "Everyone is entitled to his own opinion, but not his own facts." [134] A corollary to this statement might be "base your opinions on facts." President Trump does not ascribe to either idea.

Let's explore the differences between facts and opinion. Education needs to include both but there also needs to be education in understanding the difference. Typically someone will accept an opinion as fact if they agree with the opinion and not bother to discern whether it is a fact or pinion. I admit I do the same thing. Much of what I have written in this book is opinion but I hope that I have written my opinions in such a way that they are based on reality.

A fact is a verifiable piece of information. Example: The President in 2016 was Barack Obama. An opinion, on the other hand, is "a belief or judgment that rests on grounds insufficient to produce complete certainty or a personal view, attitude, or appraisal." [135]

In a *Time* opinion poll in August 2010 24% of the respondents said President Obama was a Muslim and only 47% believed him to be a Christian. [136] Many also believed that he was not a U. S. citizen and therefore ineligible to be President. These beliefs still persisted in 2016. Yet the facts are that Obama is an avowed Christian and was born in Hawaii, one of the United States, to a woman who was a U. S. citizen.

Opinions are the basis for decisions both great and small whether in our families, business or government. It is important therefore that opinions are based on reality and facts as well as logic to the extent possible. Our schools need to teach discernment in a consistent manner throughout the twelve years.

We also need to look at education in a different way than in the past. While reading, writing, and arithmetic served the needs of our ancestors, as our economy and society changed, new subjects were added. A common element, however, was that this education would carry the pupil through life. That is no longer true. We must emphasize from a very early age the importance of life-long learning. It will not end with high school, college, or trade school, as jobs will continue to change radically over a lifetime. This idea is very well explained in *Thank You for Being Late*, by Thomas Freedman, a columnist for the *New York Times*.

The goal in Michigan during the twentieth century was to reduce the number of school districts in order to make a more efficient system, resulting in a reduction of the number of districts from over 7,000 to 540. Now there are 294 charter schools destroying this consolidation effort.

Betsy DeVos says that schools should be able to teach anything they want. She is the first Secretary of Education who has never attended a public school and never worked in one. In November 2017 she approved a Michigan Department of Education plan for Michigan schools, which was severely flawed and opposed by our Governor and Lt. Governor and education experts.

A far better approach to universal education is to improve the public school system through cooperation rather than competition. Also needed are better teacher preparation programs and courses as well as adequate funding to meet the needs of our technological society.

Schools are important to prepare students to be educated citizens and responsible voters but just as importantly to provide people with the skills necessary to get a job that allows them to make a decent living. In this way they will purchase products and services to maintain a good life. Health care is important for this person in order to provide for himself and keep working.

A person needs good roads to get to work and other travel. The challenge is to remember that everything is interconnected.

6. Taxes Are the Dues To Be American

Oliver Wendell Holmes (1841-1935), Associate Justice of the Supreme Court 1902-1932), said, "I like to pay taxes. They are the price we pay for civilized society." [137] The Athenian model of democracy believed "those who received the greatest material benefit from being Athenians should bear the greatest burden of maintaining Athens."

Taxes provide the following services and more:
- Public education from kindergarten through college. Yes, students pay college tuition but it doesn't cover all the expenses.
- City, county and state police
- Fire protection
- Local and state libraries
- City, county, state and national parks and recreation sites
- Local, state and national highways, including rest areas, Also included is road maintenance like resurfacing, fixing pot holes, and snow removal.
- Garbage collection
- Water service
- Sewage disposal
- Various regulations, like those on utilities, food and drugs
- Jails, prisons and penitentiaries
- Social Security
- Medicare
- Aid to those in need, such as food stamps, unemployment benefits, health insurance for low income people
- Military
- Research in science and diseases
- Air traffic controllers
- National Security
- Space program
- Local, state, and federal courts
- Local, state, and federal government operations
- Federal Bureau of Investigation, and other law enforcement agencies

All of these government services and programs provide security for all citizens. This security gives us all a deeper and fuller access to the fundamental values of our country, namely the right to life, liberty, and the pursuit of happiness. They also make more real the value of equality of all citizens, also named in the Declaration of Independence.

The two taxes which affect most people the greatest are the federal income and social security taxes.

Federal Income Tax

The first national income tax (1862 to 1872) was levied to finance the Civil War. Another attempt later to institute an income tax was declared unconstitutional, so the Sixteenth Amendment was ratified in 1913 to allow an income tax. The first federal income tax in 1918 had 55 tax brackets, yet 95% of the people paid no income tax. The corporate tax rate was 12%. [138]

Simply speaking, there is still a zero tax bracket today, albeit with a relatively small number of taxpayers qualifying for it, based on family status and number of dependents. People who have no income above this bracket generally live in poverty. This zero bracket is increased through various adjustments and deductions.

In the 1960's some wealthy people were minimizing their taxes or legally avoiding the payment of taxes. Congress passed the Alternative Minimum Tax (AMT) in 1969 which required people above a certain level of income to calculate their tax by using a different method. The Tax Cuts and Jobs Act of 2017 changed the rules for the AMT so that far fewer taxpayers are subject to that tax.

David Cay Johnston wrote about the effect of tax changes between 1970 and 2000: "when the federal income tax burden on Americans overall rose by 18 percent, it fell by 16 percent for the top 400 taxpayers" and they paid a rate comparable to a single person making $123,000 or married couple with two children making $226,000. Their average income was nearly $174 million. The top 13,400 taxpayers had an average income of nearly $14 million in 2000, more than six times the average of this group in 1970." [139]

During the Reagan years (1980-1988) tax cuts became a national mantra. The primary argument for these tax cuts was the theory that cutting taxes on the wealthy would mean a great investment in our economy and thus create more jobs. All would benefit. This theory has come to be called the trickle-down economic theory, which has been proven to be ineffective in subsequent years with the great redistribution of wealth from the middle and lower income people to the wealthy. The ratio between compensation of the top CEO and the lowest paid employee has grown to five times what it was in the 1970's. People in the middle and lower income groups have actually had reduced buying power since the 1970's.

In 2001 and 2003, under President George W. Bush, taxes on the wealthy were again reduced, perpetuating the misperception that trickle-down economic policy works. These tax cuts were promoted primarily by the

Republicans but Democrats jumped on board as their wealthy supporters were benefiting from these tax cuts too. The middle class did receive reductions but they were paltry compared to the hundreds of thousands and millions of dollars the wealthy and very wealthy received.

In the 2014 election, many candidates for state office signed a pledge they would not raise taxes. This declaration is a violation of public trust. There are only two ways to provide government services and balance the budget: cut expenses or raise taxes or a combination of both. Those who pledge no tax increases hamper their ability to provide services by two-thirds. We need to elect leaders who will work at solving the problems, not add to them. The more we let the problems slide, the greater those problems become.

Income from capital gains has almost always had a special rate in the federal income tax code. In one of the tax acts, the cap on capital gains was set at 15%. This cap benefited the rich and super rich disproportionately because they have much of their income comes from these sources.

My middle class friends argue that the cap of 15% is good because it stimulates investment. For my friends, however, who make a few thousand in dividends and capital gains, the tax benefit is merely a few hundred dollars. For the super rich however, the cap is a substantial boon because two-thirds of their income comes from capital gains and dividends. So instead of paying the maximum rate of 39% on their income, their taxes are capped at 15%, a savings of 24% on millions of dollars of income.

The Tax Cut and Jobs Act of 2017 changed the income tax rates and other factors for millions of people. While it was touted as a tax cut for middle income people, it also cut taxes again for the very wealthy by millions of dollars by lowering the top rate from 39.6% to 37%. This lower rate at the top gives the top income earners hundreds of thousands and even millions of dollars in tax cuts every year. For the lower and middle class taxpayers with children, there are significant tax cuts as well. A family of four could have an income of $64,000 and pay no federal income tax with the standard deduction raised to $24,000 and tax credits of $2,000 for each child. Personal exemptions have been eliminated. The act allows 20% of self-employment income to pass tax free for some industries, including the real estate business, in which Donald Trump is heavily involved.

The Tax Cut and Jobs Act of 2017 ended the individual mandate created in the Affordable Care Act for the purpose of lowering expenses and it is expected to create a $1.5 trillion deficit in ten years. The personal tax rates and benefits are temporary but the corporate tax changes are permanent.

The net result of these changes means that most of the tax cuts again went to the wealthy. The act also raised the exemption for the federal estate tax, again benefiting only the very wealthy. One side effect that is unknown at this time is the effect this act will have on charitable contributions. There will be less tax incentive for middle income people to give to charity. Finally this act will result in adding about $1.5 trillion to the national debt. It is very irresponsible legislation.

Speaker of the House Paul Ryan was bragging abut the benefits of the act when he tweeted that a school employee had $1.50 more in her take home pay. The tweet was deleted later.

We need to adopt the saying of Oliver Wendell Holmes, "I like to pay taxes. They are the price we pay for civilized society." [140]

Social Security or Payroll Tax (FICA)

In 1935, in the midst of the Great Depression, the payroll tax (FICA) to finance Social Security was established and went into effect in 1940. Originally the plan was for retirement only but survivor benefits were added in 1939 before the plan went into effect. Disability benefits were added in 1956.

As a result of Social Security, poverty among the elderly has dropped significantly. Nearly two-thirds of those receiving Social Security benefits (including survivor and disability) count on it for more than half their income; a third rely on it for 90%". [141] Benefits are based not only on how much a person has paid in but are adjusted to benefit low income people. Hence the reason for a reduction in poverty among older people.

All wages and salaries, including self employment income, are subject to this tax. In 1954 a mere 2% of wages up to $4,200 ($84) was paid. The percent paid and the maximum dollar amounts have both increased to their current levels of 6.2% on wages up to $127,200 in 2017 with the cap increasing in ensuing years. The employer paid an equal amount until 2011 when the rate was decreased for a short time in a compromise over a government shut-down. Self-employed people pay the full rate. [142]

The total pay roll tax is 15.3% of earned income, generally on wages or salaries. This tax is equally shared by the employer and employee, with the employer's share not subject to income tax. 2.9% of this tax is for Medicare and is also shared equally by the employer and employee. The tax for Medicare has no cap.

The Social Security system has been one of the most remarkable success stories of the federal government. In 1983 Congress and the President made changes in the rate and amount of taxes paid and increased the normal retirement age to 67. As a result, the Social Security website said that there is a trust fund for Social Security benefits and "Social Security collects more in taxes than it pays in benefits. The excess is borrowed by the U.S. Treasury, which in turn issues special-issue Treasury bonds to Social Security. These bonds totaled $1.5 trillion at the beginning of 2004, and Social Security receives more than $80 billion annually in interest from them." By 2018 the surplus is estimated to be $3.6 trillion dollars.

Beginning in 2015 the benefits paid to beneficiaries have exceeded the payments made through the payroll tax. This means that the special treasury notes need to be redeemed to make up the difference. The actuarial report of the SSA projects these redemptions to average $76 billion each year between 2015 and 2018,

> *before rising steeply as income growth slows to its sustainable trend rate after the economic recovery is complete while the number of beneficiaries continues to grow at a substantially faster rate than the number of covered workers. Interest income and redemption of trust fund assets from the General Fund of the Treasury, will provide the resources needed to offset Social Security's annual aggregate cash-flow deficits until 2034. Since the cash-flow deficit will be less than interest earnings through 2019, total income will exceed expenditures and reserves of the combined trust funds will continue to grow....[143]*

Tax Reform

It makes sense to reform both the federal income tax and the payroll tax at the same time because the combined tax collected from individuals is especially high on those who make less than the maximum salary on which the payroll tax is based.

There has been much talk but little action about tax reform. Part of the problem is that the tax code is monumental and filled with loopholes which favor certain groups of people. Other factors involve the changes that have taken place over the last thirty to fifty years.

Life expectancy has increased dramatically since 1940, primarily because of the great reduction in infant mortality. At age 65, however, life expectancy is less than three years longer than it was in 1940, according to the Social Security website. If we compare the life expectancy of 21 year olds in 1940 and today, 20% more of them live to age 65. There are more than 46 million Americans over 65 compared to 9 million in 1940.

The tax burden has shifted over the years. About a hundred years ago, only 5% of the people paid income taxes. Because the Social Security tax is based on payroll and is unavoidable and withholding of income taxes is required, virtually all working people pay federal taxes today.

In 1956 28% of all federal tax revenues was from corporations. That has dropped to 10%. In 1995, 17% of the largest corporations paid no income tax. In 2017, corporations paid 9% and personal income taxpayers paid 48% of the federal government's revenue. That is expected to drop to 7% in 2018 after the Tax Cuts and Jobs Act of 2017 goes into effect. [144] In a study done by the Institute on Taxation and Economic Policy on corporate taxes paid between 2008 and 2015, very few corporations paid the 35% corporate tax rate. More than half of the profitable retail and health care companies paid an averge of more than 30%. "Among all other economic sectors, just 15 percent—less than one out of six—paid an eight-year rate exceeding 30 percent." [145]

Self-employed and higher income people have opportunities to cheat on their taxes because they are more in control of their financial situation. Corporations hire lawyers and accountants to find tax loopholes. With a strong anti-tax sentiment in this country, it is very enticing to cheat. It is estimated that billions of dollars in taxes due are not paid each year.

Most of the income for low and middle income earners comes from wages/salary, interest, and dividends, which are all reported to the Internal Revenue Service by the paying institutions, making it difficult for those taxpayers to cheat.

In addition, people are living longer, families are having fewer children so there are fewer employees in the work force paying the FICA tax.

In order to balance the budget in the 1960's President Kennedy encouraged putting FICA in the general budget. Since the government was not paying out all this tax revenue in benefits, a balanced budget resulted. That accounting procedure has resulted in attacks that Social Security recipients are receiving a dole rather than benefits based on money they and their employers paid in to the plan. This attack is, of course, utterrly false and must be rebutted whenever it comes up. The real problem is that the government is now having to buy back their notes to fund the Social Security Trust Fund so it can make payments. President Kennedy's decision to put FICA in the general budget is now coming back to haunt Congress.

Personal Income Tax Reform

In light of all these facts, one would think that the tax cuts of 2001 and 2017 would have helped the people at the bottom of the scale, since they are most adversely affected by taxes. Yet more than half of the tax benefits went to the top 1% of earners.[146]

The tax cuts of 2001, 2003, and 2017 did not change Social Security and Medicare. The tax cuts of 2017 gave the wealthy even more tax cuts.

Proposals

A guiding principle in tax reform must be: Those who benefit the most from our economic system (capitalism) are the ones who should pay the most taxes, not only in actual dollar amounts but in percentage of income.

Every now and then there is much talk about a flat income tax. At first glance, that proposal has strong appeal. Why shouldn't everyone pay the same percentage of income as tax? A flat tax is unfair because it flies against the guiding principle. For example, let's suppose the flat tax was 10%. The dollar amount is far more significant on lower incomes than on upper incomes. Ten percent of $20,000 is a hefty reduction in income and limits the person from having an adequate income, whereas ten percent of $200,000 still leaves significant income to live on and enjoy some pleasures. It is clear that more affluent people reap a far greater benefit from their taxes than low income people. For example, higher income people travel more and so use our roads more.

Michael J. Graetz in his book, *The U.S. Income Tax* (1999), proposed that we go to a value added tax (VAT) of 15-20%. This tax would generate enough revenue to make the first $90,000 of income exempt from federal income tax. This tax would eliminate the need for personal exemptions and various deductions, thus simplifying tax filing. There would be progressive tax rates for income above $90,000.

The VAT is a consumption tax used by most industrialized nations. Many states would probably oppose a VAT, since they feel consumption taxes are exclusively in their domain. Sales taxes are another form of consumption tax but are a regressive tax, affecting low wage earners the most. This is true for the same reason a flat income tax is unfair. Keep in mind, however, that low and middle income wage earners already pay a hefty flat tax for Social Security benefits.

The tax cuts of 2017 made some progress in simplifying the tax code by eliminating personal exemptions and increasing the standard deduction, but it again reduced the taxes on the wealthy. The unspoken reason for tax cuts for the wealthy is based on the false biblical "gospel of prosperity" in which God shows favor to the wealthy and so we must do that as well. Tax cuts for the wealthy are a reward. The economic arguments are purely political ones and ignore the facts that "trickle down economics" does not work. The second stage of this "gospel of prosperity" is to punish the low income and middle income people because their lack of prosperity is clearly their own fault. Speaker of the House Paul Ryan already has said the next step is to eliminate programs that help people get out of poverty or raise their financial situation.

The big problems with the federal tax code were not dealt with in 2017 including closing loopholes for the wealthy and corporations. Capital gains distributions should be taxed as ordinary income with exemptions of $2,000 per individual and $5,000 for a joint filing..The top tax rates must be increased substantially.

Reform of Social Security

The Republicans have been saying that Social Security is bankrupt and unsustainable as a pretext for getting rid of it. But the solvency of the system as described on the Social Security Administration's website shows the lie that we have been told.

However, it doesn't mean that we can ignore Social Security. There is a little hole that needs to be fixed, the fact that more benefits are being paid out each year than taxes being received. This is not a healthy situation and must be fixed by reforming the program.

I think former Senator Chuck Hagel's suggestions that the full retirement age be raised to 68 and the amount that an early retiree can receive prior to full retirement age be reduced are reasonable. These changes would go far in stabilizing the Social Security system. It also would make sense to figure benefits on a different basis, so the low income earners are truly helped. I am not in a position to actuarily determine which changes need to be made but they clearly revolve around three options or a combination of the three: raise the normal retirement age, lower the benefits, or raise taxes. Raising taxes is simple by changing the cap on earned income from $127,200 to $250,000. I prefer that all earned income be subject to the tax.

I think there should be a greater penalty for early retirement.

Another way to help the Social Security Trust Fund is for all who want to get rid of Social Security to refuse their benefits.

One of the proposals for Social Security reform during the George W. Bush administration was to replace it with personal accounts. "Private investment accounts are a terrific idea, if you can afford them and they are carefully regulated," wrote Joe Klein,[147] a political columnist, but President George W. Bush's plan failed the "social" and "security" aspects of our current system. It is not a reform of the system, but a gutting of it. This idea will certainly be raised again in 2018 and so I include some information about the private accounts here.

They take away the safety net of minimum benefits. And, of course, they will not guarantee a lifetime income, as Social Security currently does. While the market is enticing and beneficial to those with financial acumen, it would be a disaster for neophytes and the very idea is begging for disaster.

Reform of Business Taxes

The greater reform necessary revolves around corporations, how they operate and what taxes they pay or legally avoid. The 2010 Citizens United decision of the Supreme Court declared that corporations are persons and they have the right to give unlimited amounts to political campaigns anonymously. [148] The Court expanded this ruling when it gave religious freedom rights to privately held corporations in the Burwell v. Hobby Lobby decision in 2014.

If a corporation is a person, then the corporation must be taxed the same as individuals. There is no need to have a separate rate for corporations. However, if we eliminate this understanding of a corporation as a legal person, then I would be in favor of a different tax rate for corporations with a tightening of what is deductible or tax exempt. Dividends paid by a corporation should be a business deduction and fully taxable to the individual receiving the dividends. I am not opposed to the lowering of the corporate income tax rate as was done in 2017 but that decrease must be accompanied by increases in the personal income tax to offset the loss of revenue from corporations, which was not done in 2017.

Profits are one of the motives for entrepreneurs and investors. However, the ability to give benefits to executives with few restrictions must end. These perks must be taxed to the individual as ordinary income or the business should give them the salary and let them buy their own perks.

The practice that allows corporations to avoid taxes by establishing headquarters in the Cayman Islands or other offshore locations while the majority of their business is in the US must be forbidden. Billions of tax dollars are lost each year by this method of legal tax evasion.

Many businesses get tax subsidies. The list is too long to enter them all here but the oil industry is a prime example of getting billions of dollars in tax subsidies while making billions of dollars in profits. The tax cuts of 2017 will add billions of dollars to Exxon Corporation in addition to their billions of dollars of subsidies.

George W. Bush was hailed as an astute businessman for his handling of the Texas Rangers. He and a few partners bought the Rangers and made some changes. When Bush sold his share of the Rangers, he pocketed a cool $16 million on which he paid the lower capital gains tax rate rather than the regular tax rate, according to Johnston. The real kicker here, however, is that the profit made by Bush and his partners was less than the tax subsidies granted to the Rangers. In other words, we middle class taxpayers paid this profit to Bush. This is not a unique example. Subsidies for sports arenas have been occurring all over the country even though studies have shown they offer no economic benefit to a community or society.

Another form of tax subsidy is property tax abatements. We have, of course, witnessed them in Midland and they are a common business practice all over the country with one community vying against another. Cabela's has made a practice of soliciting abatements and subsidies based on projections that have been discarded by reputable economic studies. Cabela's received tax subsidies totaling $40 million, according to David Cay Johnston in *Free Lunch*, for its store in Dundee, Michigan. These subsidies include Cabela's retention of all sales taxes it collects at that store!

The Mackinac Center of Midland wrote in a report in 1989 "abatements have generally not delivered what their proponents promised." [149] The granting of tax abatements to businesses as incentives to build or expand must end across the nation. The ban would put all businesses on an even playing field. Communities could use the taxes lost to abatements to provide excellent schools and superior infrastructure, strong incentives for businesses to locate in that community.

The government policy of eminent domain, the confiscation with pay for private property for public use, has been long established in this country. The practice is used for roads especially but also for other public buildings and uses. It was used in the establishment of Sleeping Bear Dunes National Lakeshore and other public parks. It has also been used to secure land for private business.

The government's right to eminent domain was an important factor in Toledo's efforts to keep the Chrysler Jeep plant there. Chrysler stayed with the promise of "$280 million in breaks through the state's investment-tax credit and other vehicles…. The Jeep factory didn't create as many jobs as expected. It led to the destruction or removal of 83 homes and 16 businesses, including Kim's Auto and Truck Service, owned by Herman and Kim Blankenship." [150] Blankenship refused to sell and took her case all the way to the U.S. Supreme Court. Chief Justice John Roberts ruled that the case had no merit and wouldn't even hear it according to Johnston in *Free Lunch*.

The government must stop using the right of eminent domain for the purpose of giving or selling land to a potential business. Poletown in Hamtramck, Michigan stands as a stark reminder of the foolishness of such action.

As Johnston stated so well in *Free Lunch* these are all examples of "taking from the many to benefit the few." Collectively these tax breaks

102

amount to billions of dollars of lost or misspent taxes every year. As a result, there is a heavy tax burden on the middle class. When the income tax was established more than 100 years ago, it was considered morally offensive to tax an income earned by the sweat of one's brow. Now our wages are taxed to benefit the rich. It is time to change that.

Congress must give the IRS the money needed to enforce the tax laws and the tools to carry out their functions. The IRS must especially scrutinize the returns of the wealthy, who have more ways to avoid taxes, than the returns of lower income and middle income citizens, who were targeted in the late 1990's.

These tax changes would provide tax fairness. The business reforms would move us closer to free market capitalism. The challenge here is to accept taxes as dues we pay for a civilized society and then work to make sure taxes are fair. Right now the low and middle income earners pay an unfair portion of taxes which limits them from fully participating in society and the economy.

7. Foreign Policy

Instant communication and the ability to travel with ease makes our planet a much smaller place. We know what is happening on the other side of the world almost immediately. We can hop on a plane and within a day be on the other side of the world. We buy products made in places we may not even know about. Our country's foreign policy must maintain good relations with all the countries of the world because we interact with them all. They are our neighbors, even though they are thousands of miles away.

Diplomacy must be at the heart and soul of every foreign policy. Ambassadors and diplomats represent our country in foreign lands and must be very skilled and knowledgeable not only of our values and interests but also those of the countries they are working in. This knowledge includes understanding their culture and way of life, their thinking and their literature, their mode of living and their religious practices.

Sen. Chris Murphy (D-CT) summed it up this way, "To me, a progressive foreign policy is internationalist. It recognizes that America can play a role for good in the world and understands that America has to be deployed outside of our borders in order to protect ourselves from attack. A progressive foreign policy also understands that there are limits to the blunt force of military power." [151]

This internationalist element includes the support of and participation in the United Nations as a responsible partner. This involves sharing in the freedom we all want so all may have it. This partnering with the United Nations is an expansion of our security by sharing it with others.

Our foreign policy must also include the insistence on human rights, while at the same time recognizing that we are not perfect in our own guarantee of human rights. Coupled with this belief is humanitarian aid to relieve sickness and hunger, which are often the cause of unrest and civil strife.

We must support refugees, especially those who have fled from countries in civil war. While this is a contentious issue and brings about its own problems and costs, supporting refugees will enhance the view foreigners hold of the United States and will add to the richness of our culture and society.

China holds a special place in foreign policy. because most of our relationship with China involves trade. But it is important for us to have a strong ally in China for toning down the rhetoric of Kim Jung Un of North Korea, who says he has the capacity to attack the United States. We need China to defuse the potential disaster Kim Jung Un poses. President Trump is derailing our alliance with his proposed tariffs.

Security

Another consideration for a good foreign policy is security from foreign attacks and security in our daily living. This concept is usually expressed in terms of "defense" and military spending, but security comes also from diplomacy. The election of 2016 has demonstrated to us the importance of security in cyberspace. All leaders of our intelligence community testified in Congress on February 13, 2018 that Russia definitely tampered with our 2016 election and is still interfering in 2018, but our President is taking no action to stop them. He even denies that such meddling occurred or is occurring. We need a president who recognizes a threat and acts upon it in a responsible manner

The main aspect of security is defense of our country against foreign invasion. Beginning with the attack on 9/11/01, we have experienced a different kind of invasion called terrorist acts. There has been an attempt by some people to demonize Islam because some of the terrorists have been Muslims and claim Allah as their guide. Tens of thousands of peaceful Muslims are speaking out against these terrorists and are also fearful of their actions, not only upon their persons. Many Muslims fear being attacked by those who try to blame all Muslims for the actions of a few.

Robert A. Pape, University of Chicago political science scholar studied 402 suicide bombers between 1980 and 2003 and came to a conclusion that surprised him: the suicide bombers are a mix of religious and secular individuals who fear the takeover of their country and culture by outside forces. [152] It's not religious fanaticism that guides them. While terrorist attacks occur in our country, I believe the motivation is similar.

The Middle East

Israeli and Palestinian Flags

The Middle East has been a particularly troublesome area after the partitioning of the region into countries by European nations after World War I. Israel was carved out of Palestinian territory in 1948.

To make room for the Jewish immigrants, 700,000 Palestinians were forced out of their homes and land to live in foreign countries and refugee camps. The number today is estimated to be between 4 million and 7 million Palestinian people. The Palestinians have a name for this: nakba. This word should be as much a part of our vocabulary as the holocaust or shoah.

Western Wall, Dome of the Rock in Jerusalem

What Jewish settlers have done in Palestine is the same thing the European settlers did in America. They killed or forced out the Native Americans as if the new people had a divine destiny to this land. The Trail of Tears in 1838 is a grim reminder of the cruelty of the new people towards the natives.

The present leadership in Israel has made it difficult to find peace and accord with its neighbors, most especially the Palestinians. In the past great efforts were made to arrive at recognizing the Palestinian state and its right to exist. But those efforts have failed during the Obama administration, mostly because Netanyahu is very much a hardliner.

President Trump in December 2017 decided to break all precedents and ordered the American Empassy in Israel to move from Tel Aviv to Jerusalem, thus recognizing that city as the capital of Israel. Virtually all the countries of the world said it was the wrong idea and set back any peace prospects in the Middle East for a long period of time.

Assad in Syria is the most dangerous leader in the Middle East at this time and the challenge in dealing with him is very tenuous.

War

Jimmy Carter said in his acceptance speech for the 2002 Nobel Peace Prize: "War may sometimes be a necessary evil. But no matter how necessary, it is always an evil, never a good. We will not learn to live together in peace by killing each other's children."

Chris Hedges spent 15 years as a foreign correspondent, covering conflicts in Central America, the Middle East, and the Balkans. Hedges wrote about war in 2003,

> *The rush of battle is a potent and often lethal addiction, for war is a drug.... It is pedaled by mythmakers - historians, war correspondents, filmmakers, novelists, and the state - all of whom endow it with qualities it often does possess: excitement, exoticism, power, chances to rise*

above our small stations in life, and a bizarre and fantastic universe that has a grotesque and dark beauty....

Anybody who gets caught up in combat, even noncombatants, can get addicted to that rush, that sense of purpose that allows you to step outside the small daily concerns of your life and live for a great cause, to endow yourself with a kind of nobility. War is a drug - perhaps the most potent narcotic known to humankind." It is a "myth of glory, heroism, nobility" that is "sustained by the state, the entertainment industry, the press.... The biggest thing I understood is that war as it's portrayed in society is a lie. [153]

President George W. Bush appealed to that drug of patriotism when he took our country into a war of aggression in Iraq in 2003 in the aftermath of 9/11. War was a chance to make meaning of that disastrous day. War was a way to be excited again about our country. War would give us a sense of power that was damaged by the attack on this great country. And so we went to a "glorious" war to rid the world of terrorism. It was supposed to make us feel good about ourselves. It all fits Hedges' description of war.

But the war went wrong because of unfounded reasons for going to war, inadequate plans in executing the war, and a total lack of understanding of the Iraqi peoople and country. The drug that war brings to a country includes the inability to extricate itself from the war even after it has been proven to be a wrong war. For example, Sen John McCain said it would be disloyal to the soldiers who died in Iraq to pull out before it was done. This same thinking took us through the Vietnam War until over 50,000 Americans were killed.

The lie that war is glorious is perpetuated by a language of patriotism, of exalting the United States and demeaning the enemy. When that happens, it becomes very difficult to find peaceful solutions. We must not go down that road again.

Besides the financial costs of the Iraq war, we must consider also the chaos and disruption which the war caused not only in Iraq but in the entire Middle East, Europe, and the United States. We cannot afford a President who is reckless in foreign policy decisions, especially when those decisions involve war and the possibility of nuclear war.

We need to look at current situations and try to see what is happening instead of following what fits our beliefs and ideologies. As Eric Levitz, Associate Editor of Daily Intelligencer - New York Magazine, wrote in 2017, "I think that the foreign-policy establishment here sometimes continues the trend of American hubris, the belief that America alone can come up with a plan to cure the ills of foreign lands." [154]

Peacemaking

The United States military budget is "more than China, Russia, Saudi Arabia, the United Kingdom, France, India, and Germany — combined." [155] If we spent as much time, energy, and resources on peacemaking as we do on the military and confrontation, we would discover and implement the alternatives to war. But peacemaking is not just an alternative to war, it is a way of life. If we individually live as peacemakers, then we will influence others in our famly and community and we will elect people who wish to be peacemakers.

Peace is not the absence of war nor is it a situation that is enforced by the military or police. Peace is an inner harmony with oneself, one another, and, on a larger scale, with other countries. To some people, this goal may sound like a utopian dream but I believe the quest for peace is necessary at all levels and most especially at the national level. People in general are becoming more and more aware that the world is inhabited by one family. People in Asia, Africa, South America and every other place in the world are our brothers and sisters.

The obstacle to living peacefully is that we live in a culture of violence with a prevailing attitude and behaviors that encourage us to fight to resolve conflicts, to retaliate in response to attacks, and to literally fight for what we believe in. And now we have a man at the highest level of our government who has taken this low road and made it mainstream thought.

This culture of violence is taught at an early age and is reinforced in our history books. Our economic system teaches us to improve our bottom line at all costs. Our sports tell us that being number one is all that matters. Our entertainment glorifies violence in blood and gore in movies and TV shows. Our legal system promotes the rights of individuals to the neglect of the truth and compassion for victims. It would be easy to throw up our hands in despair and say "there is nothing I can do about all this."

An essential underpinning of peace on earth is the recognition that all the people on earth share a common humanity and that we need to foster a dynamic vision of difference in this unity. We are increasingly interdependent globally, which threatens the familial, religious, cultural, ethnic, and national communities that provide a sense of belonging, outlook, and promotion of their interests. An awareness of this tension can lead us to dialogue and non-violent resolution of the tension.

We need to counter and transform attitudes which encourage violence. We need to follow up the transforming attitudes with a strength of will and ability to resolve conflicts peacefully. One change in thinking we need to make is that we must work for justice, if we want peace. Justice is the key to having peace in our lives and in the world.

Very clearly, peacemaking begins with each and every one of us, right here in our local family, neighborhood, town, school, work place, and especially in our churches. Our and your efforts at peacemaking will spiral out in an ever-widening sphere of influence. With peacemaking at the center of our lives, it will influence all of our actions. For Christians, the belief in peacemaking comes right from the Gospel: be a good neighbor and love your enemies, Jesus said. I suspect most religions have similar mandates, including Islam. Actions at the heart of peacemaking include forgiveness, reconciliation, examining and getting rid of our prejudices, acting in a spirit of cooperation rather than competition, and performing acts of kindness.

There are probably few people who don't know someone from whom they are estranged in some way. The estrangement could be a result of family disputes that have lingered on for years or friends misunderstanding each other or co-workers competing for promotion. Forgiving others who make mistakes and asking for forgiveness allows us to let go of anger and resentment. It helps us heal the hurt inside. We must go a step beyond forgiveness to reconciliation with someone who has hurt us or with whom we have a misunderstanding. Reconciliation requires not only forgiveness but a reaching out to the other person. When that person accepts our reaching out, reconciliation can begin and then can conclude with the resolution of the hurts or misunderstandings. There is a peace between them. Forgiveness on the national level recognizes that the United States makes mistakes just as other countries do. So peacemaking is an individual way of life that has worldwide ramifications.

We all hold prejudices for and against various people and ideas, but we weren't born with such beliefs. As the song in *South Pacific* says, "you've got to be carefully taught" prejudices. If we were taught them, then we can unlearn them. But we must be willing to examine the prejudices very carefully, a challenging and sometimes frightening prospect. "To find the truth, you must have an unrelenting readiness to admit you may be wrong." This statement hits at the heart of prejudice. I try to live by that.

Being part of a group that recognizes everyone's talents and works together to accomplish tasks results in friendliness and camaraderie. Cooperation helps greatly to complete a project and is a natural tendency after a community disaster, like a flood, a hurricane, or the attack on 9/11. When we cooperate with others, everyone is a winner. There are no losers. Peace settles in each of us and we act differently.

Being empathic to the checkout person at a grocery store who has been on her feet for hours handling products and numbers. Being patient with the order-taker at a fast food restaurant who may be getting minimum wage and barely living from paycheck to paycheck. These actions go a long way in promoting peace among our fellow human beings.

Peacemaking by individuals has implications on the world scene. Reconciliation is at the heart of diplomacy. Recognizing our national prejudices would have allowed our country to take a different stance towards Iraq. An attitude of cooperation recognizes that the world consists of a family of nations trying to achieve the good of all. Performing acts of kindness across the world would show up in more efforts like the Peace Corps.

In 2018 we are in dire need of peacemaking efforts, especially with Donald Trump as our president. He acts like the Bully-in-Chief rather than Commander-in-Chief. He confronts everyone who disagrees with him and dismisses or taunts them. He even did so in ridiculing the leader of North Korea by calling him "little rocket man" and threatened to destroy him and his country.

The work we have to do is the same work of Rev. Reihnold Niehbuhr before and during World War II, when he promoted peace and understanding during a period of heavy anti-Semitism and other ethnic hatred, according to David Crumm of the Detroit *Free Press*. Crumm continued his column by saying that it was during this period of Niehbuhr's life that he wrote the famous Serenity Prayer. The original words go like this: "God, give us grace to accept with serenity the things that cannot be changed, courage to change the things that should be changed, and the wisdom to distinguish the one from the other."

A popular prayer and hymn says, "Let there be peace on earth and let it begin with me." Unity Church, for its annual world day of prayer in 2003, modified that prayer to read, "Let there be peace on earth and let it begin with God's love in my heart." This prayer and hymn gives us hope. There is a connection between peace in the world and me. It is a challenge to accept and believe that as well as to live by it.

8. Voting with Integrity

Citizens have had the right to vote in this country ever since we declared our independence from Great Britain. Although the ideal was present from early days, the reality is that only men were allowed to vote. Over the course of our history, the right to vote has been increased to freed men and later to women. The voting age was lowered to 18, extending voting rights to millions more people. We must exercise our right to vote in order to keep it. Many efforts over the years have resulted in keeping people from voting. Generaly these efforts are linked to racism and discrimination.

But you cannot just show up on election day and vote. Voting laws are generally state laws so the process varies from state to state. In general however the process begins with registration as a voter.

In Michigan this process is done at the local clerk's office of your city or township of residence. This is generally a simple process but it does require time and proof of identity. Once a person registers it is generally not required to register again unless the person moves to a different locality.

Traditionally an election has been held on one day from early morning to early evening but some states are now allowing multiple days for voting. If you are elderly or disabled you can obtain an absentee ballot in advance and vote in the comfort of your home. The qualifications for voting with an absentee ballot vary from state to state.

There are basically two kinds of elections. One is a proposal to levy local taxes or to amend the constitution of the state. This proposal involves voting yes or no on the question. The other kind of election chooses people to hold public office at the local, state or federal level. Within this category are two kinds of elections. The first is a primary to select a party candidate and the second is a general election to vote for the person who will actually hold office. State law regulates all elections, but candidacy requirements are subject to state and federal laws.

Our right to vote is shamefully squandered by apathy, irresponsibility, and fear. These situations, too. must be discussed so we can rise above them and actually go to the polls and vote.

Apathy can come from many sources. One is the feeling that one's vote doesn't really matter but, of course, it does. Every vote counts. Another reason for apathy is the very real challenge in grasping the issues facing our country. They are so complicated, why bother, one might say.

Close to apathy is irresponsibility. Instead of being frustrated by not knowing the issues or not caring, it is just plain irresponsible to use work as an excuse not to vote or to go on vacation or a pleasure trip. Voting under these circumstances could meanplanning ahead so vacation is not during an election day. Alternatively, a voter could apply for an absentte ballot.

Fear is a factor for minorities. A possible solution is to go with someone to the polls. Another solution for some is to get an absentee ballot. It is necessary to plan ahead for an absentee ballot, so you can receive it in time and have time to return it.

Unfortunately, the right to vote and the process involved in voting are under attack in order to restrict the right to vote. These restrictions, too, must be challenged by those of us who are unemcumbered by these restrictions.

Restrictions on voting

There have been restrictions on the right to vote from the very beginning. Women could not vote. Enslaved people could not vote. Native Americans could not vote. Males who wre not property owners could not vote in certain elections. People under age 21 could not vote. State legislators chose the United States Senators to represent their state and electors chose the President and Vice President. All of these restrictions were found in the original U. S. Constitution and, except for the last restriction, have been lifted or changed.

Since states control the voting laws, some have made it hard for certain people to vote. After the Civil War, Jim Crow laws, primarily in the Soutb made it difficult or impossible for former slaves and their descendants to vote. Those Jim Crow laws have been abolished by amendment or with the Voting Rights Act of 1965. This act was passed to ensure state and local governments do not pass laws or policies that deny American citizens the right to vote based on race. As the leading democracy of the world, the U.S. should work to keep voting free, fair, and accessible. That's why the Voting Rights Act is so important. It makes sure every citizen, regardless of their race, has an equal opportunity to have a say and participate in our great democracy.

"On June 25, 2013, the U.S. Supreme Court overturned a key provision of the Voting Rights Act, removing a critical tool to combat racial discrimination in voting. Under Section 5 of the landmark civil rights law, jurisdictions with a history of discrimination must seek pre-approval of changes in voting rules that could affect minorities. This process, known as "preclearance," blocks discrimination before it occurs. In Shelby County v. Holder, the Court invalidated Section 4 — which determines the states and localities covered by Section 5 — arguing that current conditions require a new coverage formula." [156]

Immediately some states began to take steps to restrict voting once more. "From early 2011 until the 2012 election, state lawmakers in 41 states introduced at least 180 restrictive voting bills. By the 2012 election, 19 states passed 27 restrictive voting measures, many of which were overturned or weakened by courts, citizen-led initiatives, and the Department of Justice before the election. States continued to pass voting restrictions in 2013 and 2014." [157] Restrictions on voting violate our fundamental rights to equality, life, liberty, and the pursuit of happiness.

Voter ID

A total of 13 states passed more restrictive voter ID laws between 2011 and 2014, 11 of which wre slated to be in effect in 2014. Nine states passed strict photo ID requirements, meaning a citizen cannot cast a ballot that will count without a specific kind of government-issued photo ID. An additional four states passed less strict ID requirements. Eleven percent of Americans do not have government-issued photo ID, according to a Brennan Center study, which has been confirmed by numerous independent studies. Research shows these laws disproportionately harm minorities, low-income individuals, seniors, students, and people with disabilities. In Texas, for example, early data from the state showed that between 600,000 and 800,000 registered voters did not have the kind of photo ID required by the state's law, and that Hispanics were 46 to 120 percent more likely to lack an ID than whites. In North Carolina, estimates show that 318,000 registered voters — one-third of whom are African-American — lack a DMV-issued ID.

Voter Registration

Between 2011 and 2014 a total of nine states passed laws making it harder for citizens to register to vote. These measures took a variety of forms.

Four states have new restrictions on voter registration drives. Nationally, African-Americans and Hispanics register through drives at twice the rate as whites. Three states also passed laws requiring registrants to provide documentary proof of citizenship, which as many as 7 percent of Americans do not have readily available. North Carolina eliminated highly popular same-day registration, and Wisconsin made it harder for people who have moved to stay registered.

Early Voting

Eight states passed laws cutting back on early voting days and hours. These restrictions could exacerbate lines on Election Day and are particularly likely to hurt minority voters. For example, in North Carolina, Department of Justice data show that 7 in 10 African-Americans who cast ballots in 2008 voted during the early voting period, and 23 percent of them did so during the week that was cut. Many states eliminated weekend and evening hours, when minority voters are more likely to cast a ballot. According to a study in Ohio in 2008, 56 percent of weekend voters in Cuyahoga County, the state's most populous, were black.

Restoring Voting Rights to Felons

Three states also made it harder to restore voting rights for people with past criminal convictions. These laws disproportionately impact African-Americans. Nationwide, 7.7 percent of African-Americans have lost the right to vote, compared to 1.8 percent of the rest of the population. [158]

Gerrymandering

Every ten years the state legislatures draw new boundaries for the U. S. Congressional districts and the state legislative districts because of the population changes in the country. These changes are based on the census which is conducted every ten years by the United States government.

In the early 19th century Governor Elbridge Gerry of Massachusetts was instrumental in drawing up boundaries for these districts in such a way that they looked like salamanders. Ever since then the word gerrymander has been used to refer to the manipulation of these new districts so as to benefit the party in power. Both parties have done it but in the last several redistrictings, the practice has been widespread. Couple this with the very strong Tea Party and Republican efforts at the local level and it results in more state legislatures and governors becoming Republican, even in states which are traditionally Democratic in national elections, such as Michigan. This state has a very large majority Republican House and Senate as well as a Republican governor, but has two U. S. Democratic Senators and voted for Democrat Obama twice. Michigan voted for Trump by a mere 10,000 votes.

The Electoral College

The original purpose of the Electoral College was to elect honorable independent men who would choose the President. The framers of the Constitution held this position in such high honor they did not want it to be filled without serious consideration. This original purpose has been subverted over the course of history and must be changed or ended.

Article II, Section 1 of the Constitution says in part "Each State shall appoint, in such Manner as the Legislature thereof may direct, a Number of Electors, equal to the whole Number of Senators and Representatives to which the State may be entitled in the Congress."

In 1788 James Madison, Alexander Hamilton, and John Jay wrote a series of essays, called the Federalist papers, in defense of the newly created Constitution. In No. 68 Hamilton wrote that the meeting of the electoral college "affords a moral certainty, that the office of President will never fall to the lot of any man who is not in an eminent degree endowed with the requisite qualifications," [159] because they were independent men chosen expressly for this purpose.

Originally, the President and Vice-President did not run as a team but rather the one with the most electoral votes became President and the second became the Vice-President. In 1800, the electoral vote was a tie, so the House of Representatives broke the tie.

In 1824 there were four candidates for President. The independent electors could not agree on which one to elect so the decision went again to the House of Representatives which chose John Quincy Adams.

Gradually over the course of the nineteenth century, political parties gained more and more control over the electoral process and states began to allow the people to vote for president. It should be noted that South Carolina did not have a popular vote for president until after the Civil War. [160]

The debate over whether the people should elect the president or continue to use the Electoral College process began and continues to this day. Four elections resulted in the electoral college voting for a candidate who had fewer popular votes: 1876, 1888, 2000, and 2016. [161] [162]

States controlled whom they appointed electors and when they met , many times over a period of months. [163] [164] By the beginning of the twentieth century, it was a widespread practice for political parties to choose the electors rather than the state legislature.

The United States Supreme Court ruled in Ray v. Blair in 1952 that a political party can demand that its electors promise to vote for the candidate the party wants. In 29 states the electors are mandated by law to vote for the winner of the popular vote in their state. Not only are the electors no longer independent, the winner of a state gets all the electoral votes, except in Maine and Nebraska. [165]

Prior to 1964 many states had a legislature modeled after the U. S. Congress: one house based on population and the other based on geographical areas. In 1964 the Supreme Court, applying the Equal Protection Clause of the U.S. Constitution, ruled in Reynolds v. Sims that both houses of state legislatures needed to be based on population, not geographical areas. This is often referred to as the "one man one vote" principle. [166] While the Electoral College is part of the Constitution, it clearly violates the principle established in Reynolds v. Sims. Because of the way electoral votes are assigned, popular votes are not equal around the country. In 2016 Wyoming had 3 electoral votes with a population of 585,501. This means each vote represented 195,167 people. On the other hand, California had a population of 39,250,000 with 55 electoral votes. Each vote represented 713,616 people. This means that Wyoming votes were worth nearly four times the votes in California. [167]

The thirteen original states were made up of distinct groups of people for the most part and their sovereignty was recognized. Today the sovereignty of the individual states is nearly irrelevant as migration constantly changes the population and traditions of states. While I was born and raised in Michigan and have lived most of my life here, I would be at home just as easily in many other states.

Renewed interest in how the Electoral College works (or doesn't work) occurred after Donald Trump won the presidency even though Hilary Clinton received nearly 3 million more popular votes. Efforts at urging the electors to abandon their pledge to vote for Trump was rooted in the original intent of the framers of the Constitution. However, the electors do not cast their vote based on an independent appraisal of the candidate but rather on their pledge to a political party. [168]

It is clearly time to accept the results of the popular vote. This can be done through state legislation since states control the Electoral College. Ten states and the District of Columbia have already passed legislation requiring their electors to vote for the winner of the national popular vote (The National Popular Vote plan). These states represent 165 electoral votes, 105 short of the 270 needed to win an election. When states which have passed such legislation total 270 electoral votes, the law will take effect. [169]

Donald Trump, before he was elected President, and Newt Gingrich have both expressed disdain for the Electoral College and support the National Popular Vote Plan. [170]

Other options to "fix" the Electoral College is to have proportional allocation of electoral votes based on the popular vote in each state and would require states to pass a law. Another proposal is to eliminate the electoral college and depend on the popular vote, which requires a Constitutional amendment.

116

Reform of voting procedures

With a very mobile society, it makes sense that the rules for registering to vote must be easy, brief, and transparent. Since the voting age has been lowered to 18, it is important that students not be barred from registering.

Elections for national office could be held over several days as happened in Florida in 2008 but the last day would be set up so that the polls close at the same time all over the country except in Hawaii. In this way there would be no results posted early to influence later voters, except in Hawaii. In order to encourage voting, even local elections could be held on more than one day. Requiring people to vote is another option that would get people to vote. Making election day a holiday could also help bring out the voters but I fear many would just take it as a vacation day.

The campaign for election, especially for President, is far too long and far too costly. As a result, only the wealthiest are generaly able to mount a serious campaign for national office. As I was writing this part of the book in the summer of 2015, candidates for President were already campaigning and we had already engaged in one debate. The election was still 15 months away! Now in 2016 I have observed the most disturbing presidential campaign in my lifetime. Campaigns for office should begin no earlier than six months prior to the election. Local elections are generally not a problem in this regard but state and national campaigns stretch out over too long a period. Our elected leaders need to do their job, not campaign for office.

A shorter time frame would allow anyone with serious credentials to get his/her name in front of the people. Requirements for a candidate to get on the ballot need to be open enough so that "third party" candidates (even fourth and fifth party) would have easy access to the ballot. Once the requirements are met, all candidates would have public funding for their campaign and could spend no more. Various public debates and town hall meetings for each office would be televised for all constituents to watch and/or listen to.

Technology is a wonderful modern tool to make life easier and offers a more efficient use of time with results produced in seconds or minutes. Voting technology gives us all these benefits too. The Help America Vote Act of 2002 ordered some changes in voting after the debacle of 2000 but it failed in one very important aspect. It allowed paperless electronic voting machines. This means there is no way to have a recount but more importantly there is no way to record votes in the case of computer failure. And all who have computers have experienced computer failures. Even more significantly perhaps is the possibility of fraud inherent in such machines. A programmer or hacker could change the code to produce results just different enough to make the loser a winner. Voting is such a sacred right that the paperless voting machines must be done away with. In 2009 17 states and DC were still using paperless voting machines. Fortunately Michigan is not one of them. [171] In 2016 only Georgia, Delaware, Louisiana, New Jersey, and South Carolina used paperless machines but there were still others using machines that were easily hackable, according to Edward Felton, professor of computer science at Princeton.[172]   Russian hackers tried to infiltrate voting machines in at least 21 states, according to the Department of Homeland security.[173]

The problem of paperless voting machines is only the tip of the iceberg, according to the Brennan Center for Justice. The real problem is aging machines in dozens of states, which are based on a platform that is at the end or near the end of its projected life. "In 14 states, machines are 15 or more years old."The problem is decrepit electronics can misrecord votes, lose votes en masse because of faulty memory, and be hacked at the tabulation stage by insiders who know it takes very little to swing close races." Many of these machines have no paper trail. "The biggest risk is increased failures and crashes, which can lead to long lines and lost votes." [174]

There must be uniform rules regarding the number of machines per registered voters around the country. ID requirements must be as lenient as possible. Changing the rules this way would bring about several significant benefits. The process would have more credibility and voters would have more options in a more disciplined manner. The candidates would be on an equal footing even third party candidates who seldom can make it in the current process.

We need to place more emphasis on not only the electoral process but what is at stake in that process. It is unconscionable that in the best country in the world we marvel at 60% turnout in a presidential election. Contests in the recent Michigan primary election were decided by less than 25% of registered voters. Local elections quite often have the shameful turnout of merely 3-5%. These statistics don't even take into account the number of citizens who have not bothered to register. Many people complain about the quality of candidates for public office but we have only ourselves to blame. The less citizen participation in the electoral process means the greater possibility of poorly qualified candidates.

Finally, it is of extreme importance that the United States prevent Russia and other foreign countries from meddling in our electoral process. Directors of the various intelligence agencies of the federal government testitied in Congress on February 13, 2018 that such meddling took place in 2016 and is continuing but nothing is being done to stop it from occurring in 2018.

Several challenges come from this chapter. One is to make it a top priority to vote in every election. The more difficult challenge is to be aware of the issues and vote responsibly. Underneath these two challenges is the challenge to make sure the right to vote is guaranteed to all voters.

9. The General Welfare

This last chapter is perhaps the most important one in this book because it is here where you, the reader, come to some conclusions about how you will vote. The one element that ties all the chapters together is the general welfare of our country as stipulated in our Constitution. Another way to describe this is "the common good". Let me illustrate the common good by giving examples of the opposite.

The Family Circus cartoon often shows the children standing in front of Mom and saying "Not me" when she questions them about a broken vase or toy. While we may think it is cute in the comics, it can be frustrating to parents in real life. When adults have this attitude, it definitely is problematic.

Not only do people wish to push the blame away from them to protect their integrity or good name, but they also want to avoid responsibility. The problem shows up in local, state, and national issues.

Several years ago, when the former Regina High School in Midland, Michigan was up for sale, a group had an interest in making it a home for the developmentally challenged. "That's a good idea, but not in my neighborhood," people said.

We live in a time of great financial stress on all levels of government. Very few people are willing to talk about increasing taxes because the momentum is in the other direction, irresponsible as that is. Jennifer Granholm, Governor of Michigan (2003-2011), suggested a tax on services. "Not my services," was heard from almost all sectors of the service economy.

Local school boards in Michigan are trying to resolve a tremendous budget shortfall by the only means they have available: cutting services. "Not the janitors", some say; "not my child's teacher", others say; "not my sport", still others say. Due to the now infamous Proposal A that shifted property taxes to the state for distribution, local school boards in Michigan no longer have the option of raising taxes for operation.

The epitome of the "not me" attitude is fighting a war with borrowed money instead of taxing people for it. That is bad enough, but the reality is that taxes in 2003 were actually reduced and disproportionately reduced on those who could best afford to pay the taxes that would finance the war in Iraq many of them so strongly supported. Again, "don't raise my taxes", they said.

One would think that building schools and churches are exempt from this attitude, but they are not. When schools and churches are proposed for a certain location., neighbors have complained that they don't want the land used for the large parking space that would be required for a church, or the increased traffic for either one, so once again we hear "not in my neighborhood."

People move to the country to get out into the open spaces. Then they complain about the smell from the neighboring pig farm and want the farmer to move! Or they complain about a developer who comes along and subdivides the surrounding land. They complain they are losing their country culture and becoming a subdivision – exacly what they moved into the country to get away from. And so have all the others who moved in around them. "No development in my neighborhood", they say.

While there is no precise definition for the general welfare or the common good, it does mean that citizens need to have a view on issues that looks at how an issue affects the general population, not just their own interests. It is not equivalent to "majority rule". Rather, the common good always takes into consideration the impact on minorities and those left out of the mainstream.

The common good is "the sum of those conditions of social life which allow social groups and their individual members relatively thorough and ready access to their own fulfilment".[175] Adequate housing and transportation are key elements, wrote Pope Francis. [176]

In the case of Regina High School, the concern should not have been fear of the residents of the proposed home or potential loss of property values, but whether the site was suitable for such a community home.

Taxes are not something bad, but rather the way we provide common services, like education, roads, police and fire protection. Michigan can't just cancel taxes and expect to have a vibrant place to live. Midland Public Schools cannot operate on a deficit budget so services must be cut or changed. The common good question is "which cuts meet the best interestes of most students and the community". That question is being asked all around Michigan. To compound the need to provide quality education in Michigan, the state Department of Education and the state legislature are ignoring the terrible test results from all across Michigan.

There are two very serious obstacles to looking at the common good. Both obstacles impact one's integrity. One is extreme ideologies that guides so many people who are unwilling to compromise, and view compromise as a sign of weakness. They defend their positions as if they have been given to them directly by God. Such people are found on both the right and left of the political and social spectra.

A subset of an extreme ideology is the voice of the National Rifle Association (NRA). All the leadership can see is their right to own arms, disregarding the consequences of so many wepons that are easily available. When ideology stands in the way of human compassion, it is extreme and must be challenged. The NRA represents such a view. After the shootings in

San Bernardino, a spokesman for the NRA said that California has the toughest gun laws in the country and they didn't prevent these shootings. [177] The implication is we don't need more laws. But the NRA offered nothing to stop the shootings except urging people to have more guns.

After one of the worst mass shootings in American history occurred on June 12, 2016 in Orlando, Florida, Republicans refused to even hold a vote on universal background checks or keep potential terrorists from buying assault weapons. Paul Ryan, Speaker of the House, said he would not call for a vote on a bill that denies constitutional rights withut due process. One could interpret this action to mean that the Second Amendment has no limits and that it is okay for anyone to buy arms, even weapons of war like assault rifles. The NRA stance on guns is an example of extreme ideology and must be challenged as a barrier to the common good.

The same opposition to reasonable gun controls followed the worst mass shooting in Las Vegas in 2017. I keep wondering after these events if this is the one that will force our legislatures to act responsibly. On February 14, the 6th school shooting of 2018 occurred in Florida. Will this tragedy move people to act responsiblyt?

Another subset of extreme ideology is religious fundamentalism, which occurs in all the major religions. Any religion which preaches and practices intolerance, hatred, racism, and/or murder is not authentic and should be curtailed. Pope Francis remarked after the shootings in Paris in 2015 that to claim that massacre as the will of God is blasphemy.

Another obstacle to seeking the common good is the cultural and social reality which says that being white is superior and being male is superior. This obstacle applies to white males who have an advantage merely because of those two characteristics. It is very easy to think that my achievements have been solely the result of my efforts but white privilege has its advantages and must be examined by everyone. We must oppose the white supremacy movement that has become mainstream under President Trump and his allies.

Seeking the common good necessarily means that our votes must be based on multiple considerations. Voting based on one issue is contrary to the common good although one of many issues could make one candidate more preferable than another

There are some Catholic groups who insist that there are some issues that are non-negotiable. The list is often so long that no candidate would qualify for one's vote. In this case, I agree with the Catholic bishops, who wrote in their quadrennial letter on faithful citizenship that one must make a prudential choice for the one who most likely will support the common good.

Many leaders and potential leaders claim the United States to be a Christian country. The Bible is the foundational book for Christian beliefs and practices. It is also a sacred book for Muslims. The Hebrew Scriptures, generally our Old Testament, is the holy writings of the Jews. With this in mind, I wish to end this book with a quote from the prophet Isaiah. It is a message which I feel will sit well with those who are not of the Abrahamic tradition.

Thus says the Lord GOD:
Cry out full-throated and unsparingly,
lift up your voice like a trumpet blast;
Tell my people their wickedness,
and the house of Jacob their sins.
They seek me day after day,
and desire to know my ways,
Like a nation that has done what is just
and not abandoned the law of their God;
They ask me to declare what is due them,
pleased to gain access to God.
"Why do we fast, and you do not see it?
afflict ourselves, and you take no note of it?"

Lo, on your fast day you carry out your own pursuits,
and drive all your laborers.
Yes, your fast ends in quarreling and fighting,
striking with wicked claw.
Would that today you might fast
so as to make your voice heard on high!
Is this the manner of fasting I wish,
of keeping a day of penance:
That a man bow his head like a reed
and lie in sackcloth and ashes?
Do you call this a fast,
a day acceptable to the LORD?
This, rather, is the fasting that I wish:
releasing those bound unjustly,
untying the thongs of the yoke;
Setting free the oppressed,
breaking every yoke;
Sharing your bread with the hungry,
sheltering the oppressed and the homeless;
Clothing the naked when you see them,
and not turning your back on your own.
Then your light shall break forth like the dawn,
and your wound shall quickly be healed;

122

This is the common good.

About the Author

Norbert Bufka was born and raised on a small farm in northern Michigan. He graduated from St. Joseph's Seminary in Grand Rapids. He earned a BA in history at Aquinas College, a MA in Latin at Illinois State, and a Master of Pastoral Studies degree from Loyola University New Orleans.

Bufka has written numerous letters to the editor, over 100 op-ed columns for the Midland Daily News, and 14 books.   His favorite topics are history, religion, and Pope Francis. He has given many talks at his local parish.

In 2017 Bufka joined others to form the Michigan Center for Progressive Public Policy (MCP3) in order to advocate for progressive values and policies.

Books by Norbert Bufka
Pope Francis series
Pope Francis: The Beginning of a New Era
Jesus and Pope Francis: Models for Living
A Study Guide for "Joy of the Gospel" by Pope Francis
"The Care of Our Common Home" by Pope Francis: A Study Guide
"The Joy of Love" by Pope Francis: Full Text, Commentaries, Implementation, and Study Guide

Leelanau Series:
From Bohemia to Good Harbor: The Story of the Bufka Family in Leelanau County, Michigan
Good Harbor, Michigan: The Story and the People 1850-1931
News from the Neighborhood: Good Harbor, Michigan 1875-1931
North Unity and Bohemian Settlement

Other books:
The Nicene Creed: A Reinterpretation
Saint Joseph's Seminary: Personal and Historical Perspectives
The Rosary: Traditional and Alternative Mysteries
Being Catholic, Becoming Faithful

These books are available from the author at https://www.thisonly.org and Amazon..

Bibliography

"The 35% Corporate Tax Myth", https://itep.org/the-35-percent-corporate-tax-myth/

Allen, Karma, Emily Shapiro, and Julia Jacobo, "Las Vegas shooting death toll rises to 59, no apparent connection to international terror", *ABC News*, http://abcnews.go.com/US/las-vegas-shooting-death-toll-rises-59-apparent/story?id=50223240.

American Family Association, Press Release. April 16, 2015. http://www.afa.net/who-is-afa/press-releases/2015/04-april/american-family-association-attacks-on-religious-freedom-underscore-why-protections-are-needed/

Arbinger Institute, *The Anatomy of Peace: Resolving the Heart of Conflict*. San Francisco: Berrett-Koehler Publishers, Inc., 2006.

Arrigo, Barbara, "Defending Social Security system begins with history lesson", *The Detroit Free Press*, March 28, 2005.

Boswell, John, Christianity, Social Tolerance, and Homosexuality: Gay People in Western Europe from the beginning of the Christian era to the 14th century, Chicago: University of Chicago Press, 1980.

Blythe, Anne, "A judge, a Vegas phone call and the NC GOP legislative effort to remake the judicial branch", The News & Observer, August 22, 2017. http://www.newsobserver.com/news/politics-government/state-politics/article168661047.html

Brennan Center for Justice https://www.brennancenter.org/issues/restricting-vote

"Bush Proposal Differs Greatly from Model", *Washington Post*, March 3, 2005.

Bustillo, Miguel. "Shooting ok", , *the Los Angeles Times*, July 08, 2008. http://www.latimes.com/news/nationworld/nation/la-na-shoot1-2008jul01,0,2089276.story

Cahill, Teddy, Wesley Lowery and Niraj Chokshi , "Calls for calm after grand jury declines to indict officers in death of Tamir Rice", *The Washington Post*, December 29, 2015. https://www.washingtonpost.com/news/post-nation/wp/2015/12/28/tamir-rice-grand-jury-announcement-expected-monday/?wpmm=1&wpisrc=nl_evening

Chernow, Ron, *Alexander Hamilton,* New York: Penguin Group, 2004.

Chernow, Ron, *Grant,* New York: Penguin Press, Bookshare, 2017.

Clinton, Hillary Rodham, *What Happened*, New York: Simon & Schuster, Bookshare, 2017.

Cohen, John and Kyle Dropp, "Most Americans object to planned Islamic center near Ground Zero, poll finds", *Washington Post*, September 9, 2010. http://www.washingtonpost.com/wp-dyn/content/article/2010/09/08/AR2010090806231.html?wpisrc=nl_headline

"Crime in 2017: A Preliminary Analysis", Brennan Center for Justice for All, https://www.brennancenter.org/publication/crime-2017-preliminary-analysis

"Current U.S. Federal Government Tax Revenue", https://www.thebalance.com/current-u-s-federal-government-tax-revenue-3305762

Dickey, Jay and Mark Rosenberg, "How to protect gun rights while reducing the toll of gun violence", Washington Post, December 25, 2015. https://www.washingtonpost.com/opinions/time-for-collaboration-on-gun-research/2015/12/25/f989cd1a-a819-11e5-bff5-905b92f5f94b_story.html

"Drug ads: $5.2 billion annually -- and rising" CBS, https://www.cbsnews.com/news/drug-ads-5-2-billion-annually-and-rising/.

Eddlem, Thomas R., *Meet the Author of U.S. Constitution's Preamble Learn about 18th-century statesman patriot Gouverneur Morris*, http://www.america.gov/st/pubs-english/2006/April/20060403182030pssnikwad0.6276056.html#ixzz0IPpuwaQp&D

"The Fair Sentencing Act", *Wikipedia*, https://en.wikipedia.org/wiki/Fair_Sentencing_Act

Flake, Jeff, *Conscience of a Conservative: A Rejection of Destructive Politics and a Return to Principle*, New York, Random House, Bookshare, 2017.

Ford, Zack, "The True Intent Of Indiana's 'Religious Freedom' Bill, According To The People Who Helped Write It", March 31, 2015. http://thinkprogress.org/lgbt/2015/03/31/3640801/conservatives-indiana-discrimination/

Francis, *The Care of Our Common Home*, (*Laudato Si)* Libreria Editrice Vaticana, 2015.

Gellman, Barton and Arshad Mohammed, "NSA call database explained", *Washington Post* May 12, 2006. http://everything.explained.today/NSA_call_database/

Graetz, Michael J. *The U.S. Income Tax*, New York: W. W. Norton & Company, 1999.

Guarino, Mark. "Why a dash-cam video of a police shooting might not be a smoking gun", *The Washington Post*, December 28, 2015.

https://www.washingtonpost.com/national/why-a-dash-cam-video-of-a-police-shooting-might-not-be-a-smoking-gun/2015/12/28/9e0f8cda-ad7e-11e5-9ab0-884d1cc4b33e_story.html?wpmm=1&wpisrc=nl_evening

"Gun related deaths keep Going Up", http://time.com/5011599/gun-deaths-rate-america-cdc-data", http://time.com/5011599/gun-deaths-rate-america-cdc-data/.

"Gun violence in the United States", *Wikipedia*, https://en.wikipedia.org/wiki/Gun_violence_in_the_United_States

Hedges, Chris, War is a Force that Gives Us Meaning,

Holmes, Oliver Wendell, "Taxes Are What We Pay for Civilized Society", *Quote Investigator*, http://quoteinvestigator.com/2012/04/13/taxes-civilize/

Hohmann, James, "THE BIG IDEA: Donald Trump celebrated Sunday that his campaign to delegitimize the free press is working", *The Washington Post*, October 24, 2017.

"How bad is US gun violence?", *The Guardian*, https://www.theguardian.com/us-news/2017/oct/05/us-gun-violence-charts-data.

"Incarceration in the United States", *Wikipedia*, https://en.wikipedia.org/wiki/Incarceration_in_the_United_States

"Infrastructure", *Wikipedia*, https://en.wikipedia.org/wiki/Infrastructure

Ingraham, Christopher. "27 Americans were shot and killed on Christmas day", *The Washington Post*, December 28, 2015. https://www.washingtonpost.com/news/wonk/wp/2015/12/28/guns-killed-more-people-on-christmas-in-the-u-s-than-in-an-entire-year-in-these-countries/?wpmm=1&wpisrc=nl_evening

"Is There Really A Crisis?, *Time*, January 24, 2015, http://content.time.com/time/magazine/0,9263,7601050124,00.html

Jenkins, Nash, "Exclusive: Sen. Jeff Flake Defends His 'Yes' Vote on the Republican Tax Bill", *Time*, December 6, 2017, http://time.com/5052680/jeff-flake-gop-tax-reform-deficit/.

Johnston, David Cay. Free Lunch: How the Wealthiest Americans Enrich Themselves at Government Expense (and Stick You with the Bill), New York: Penguin Group, 2007

Johnston, David Cay. Perfectly Legal: The Covert Campaign to Rig Our Tax System to Benefit the Super-Rich -- and Cheat Everyone Else, New York: Penguin Books, 2003.

Kadlec, Daniel, "The New Tax Trap", *Time*, March 28, 2005.

Kaffer, Nancy, "How to work on gun violence without violating the Second Amendment", Detroit *Free Press*, June 15, 2016. http://www.freep.com/story/opinion/columnists/nancy-kaffer/2016/06/15/atf-orlando-reform/85867932/

Kaza, Greg and Dr. Gary L. Wolfram "Property Tax Abatements", Mackinac Center, Posted: June 1, 1989, http://www.mackinaw.org/article.aspx?ID=6244

Kinsley, Michael, "Kidding Ourselves About Immigration", *Time*, December 6, 2007.

Klein, Joe, "Social Security: How Would the Bush Plan Work?", *Time,* January 24, 2005, http://content.time.com/time/magazine/0,9263,7601050124,00.html

Kendi, Ibram X., *Stamped From The Beginning: The Definitive History Of Racist Ideas In America*, Bookshare, 2016.

Krakauer, Steve, Gingrich Compares Ground Zero Mosque To 'Nazi Sign Next To Holocaust Museum' August 16, 2010. http://www.mediaite.com/online/newt-gingrich-compares-ground-zero-islamic-center-to-nazi-sign-next-to-holocaust-museum/

Lakoff, George, The ALL NEW Don't Think of an Elephant! Vermont: Chelsea Green Publishing, 2004, 2014.

Lewis, Charles and Bill Allison and the Center for Public Integrity, *The Cheating of America*, William Morrow, 2001.

Levin, Mark R., *Rediscovering Americanism: And the Tyranny of Progressivism*.Bookshare, 2017.

Levitz, Eric, "Progressives Need a New Foreign Policy Vision. This Democratic Senator Says He Has One", *NYMagazine*, May 7, 2017. http://nymag.com/daily/intelligencer/2017/05/this-senator-wants-to-make-foreign-policy-progressive-again.html.

"Lobbying Spending Data Base– Pharmaceuticals Health Products 2017", Open Secrets https://www.opensecrets.org/lobby/indusclient.php?id=h04.

Lowery, Wesley. "DOJ will investigate July death of Darrius Stewart, an unarmed, black 19-year-old shot by police in Memphis", *The Washington Post*, December 14, 2015. https://www.washingtonpost.com/news/post-nation/wp/2015/12/14/doj-will-investigate-july-death-of-darrius-stewart-an-unarmed-black-19-year-old-shot-by-police-in-memphis/

"Madoff whistle-blower attacks SEC", *BBC News*, February 5, 2009. http://news.bbc.co.uk/go/pr/fr/-/2/hi/business/7871253.stm

"Mass Incarceration – the whole pie 2017", Prison Policy Initiative, https://www.prisonpolicy.org/reports/pie2017.html

Mayer, Jane, "Covert Operations: The billionaire brothers who are waging a war against Obama", *The New Yorker* August 30, 2010. http://www.newyorker.com/reporting/2010/08/30/100830fa_fact_mayer?printable=true#ixzz0xlrkH100

"Mass shooting", *Wikipedia*, https://en.wikipedia.org/wiki/Mass_shootings_in_the_United_States

The three most deadly have occurred between June 2016 and November 2017, a seventeen month. "

Muslim Americans Under Attack As Far Right Fights To Deny Them From Building Their Own Places Of Worship", *Think Progress*, March 26, 2010. http://thinkprogress.org/2010/05/26/muslim-americans-right-worship/ May 26, 2010.

"New Agenda Outlines Ways Congress, Administration Can Act on Criminal Justice Reform", https://www.brennancenter.org/press-release/new-agenda-outlines-ways-congress-administration-can-act-criminal-justice-reform, May 15, 2017..

"Obergefell v. Hodges", *Wikipedia*, https://en.wikipedia.org/wiki/Obergefell_v._Hodges.

Ortiz, Erik, "Walmart Shooting in Thornton, Colorado: Suspect Scott Ostrem Is Arrested", *NBC News*, November 2, 2017. https://www.nbcnews.com/news/us-news/gunman-kills-3-walmart-thornton-colorado-n816746.

Parvez Ahmed, "What Would Our Founding Fathers Say About the 'Ground Zero Mosque'?", *The Huffington Post*, August 23, 2010

"Penal Reform International", https://www.penalreform.org/priorities/prison-conditions/issue/

Pitts, Jr. Leonard, "Beck's exploitation of struggle is obscene", August 27, 2010. http://rocnow.com/article/opinion-syndicated-columns/20108270338

Pitts Jr., Leonard, "Public silence greets poor's powerlessness", *Miami Herald*, February 2, 2010. http://www.miamiherald.com/living/columnists/leonard-pitts/story/1454250.html

"Police Shootings", *The Washington Post*",retrieved January 5, 2016. https://www.washingtonpost.com/graphics/national/police-shootings/

Powers, Elia, "Wrangling Over Unit Records". July 7, 2006. https://www.insidehighered.com/news/2006/07/07/unitrecord

"Prison Conditions in the United States of America:, *Human Rights Watch*, https://www.hrw.org/legacy/advocacy/prisons/u-s.htm

"Republicans Float Ideas for Social Security", *Washington Post,*March 6, 2005.

"Republicans Push for Sentencing Reform ", Brennan Center for Justice, http://www.brennancenter.org/newsletter/justice-update-president-misleads-crime-republicans-push-sentencing-reform

"Rivals shape public message", *The Detroit News*, March 27, 2005.

Rosenfeld, Steven, "A Voting Machine Meltdown in 2016 Is Likely, Investigation Warns", *Alternet*, September 18, 2015.

http://www.alternet.org/election-2016/voting-machine-meltdown-2016-likely-investigation-warns

Schoenherr, Neil, "Cost of incarceration in the U.S. more than $1 trillion", September 7, 2016..https://source.wustl.edu/2016/09/cost-incarceration-u-s-1-trillion/.

Schulberg, Jessica, "Good News for Russia, 15 states use easily hackable voting machines", *Huffington Post*, July 17, 2017. https://www.huffingtonpost.com/entry/electronic-voting-machines-hack-russia_us_5967e1c2e4b03389bb162c96.

Shank, Duane. "Reform, Reduce, Destroy", *Sojourners Magazine,* April 2005. http://sojo.net/magazine/2005/04/reform-reduce-destroy

Shearer, Michael, "Seven things that could go wrong on election day", *Time*, October 23, 2008. http://www.truthout.org/102508A

Shlaes, Amity. When Chrysler's Jeep Runs Over the Little Guy, March 1, 2006. http://www.bloomberg.com/apps/news?pid=newsarchive&sid=aYbnXJNIe0VA

"Social Security ills divide aging Mich.", The Detroit News, March 27, 2005.

"Status of the Social Security and Medicare Programs", https://www.ssa.gov/oact/

Stockman, Dan, "Dick's Sporting Goods' gun policy change followed sister talks", *NCROnline*, March 1, 2018. ,http://globalsistersreport.org/news/ministry/dicks-sporting-goods-gun-policy-change-followed-sister-talks-52301.

Thandeka , The Cost of Whiteness, http://www.afrocentricnews.com/html/cost_of_whiteness.html

"TIME Poll: Majority Opposes Mosque, Many Distrust Muslims", *Time*, August 19, 2010. http://www.time.com/time/nation/article/0,8599,2011799,00.html?xid=newsletter-daily

"United States incarceration rate", *Wikipedia*, https://en.wikipedia.org/wiki/United_States_incarceration_rate

Weigel, David "Alabama tried a Donald Trump-style immigration law. It failed in a big way." *Washington Post*, August 22, 2015. http://www.washingtonpost.com/politics/alabama-tried-a-donald-trump-style-immigration-law-it-failed-in-a-big-way/2015/08/22/2ae239a6-48f2-11e5-846d-02792f854297_story.html?wpmm=1&wpisrc=nl_headlines

Weinberg, Neil, Michael Maiello and David K. Randall, , *Forbes,* May 19, 2008. http://www.forbes.com/forbes/2008/0519/114.html?boxes=custom

Williams, Robertson, "Caught Again by the AMT", Forbes, https://www.forbes.com/sites/beltway/2017/05/12/caught-again-by-the-amt/#2efc525e26dc.

Wheeler, Lydia, "Supreme Court strikes down NC districts as illegally based on race", May 22, 2017. http://thehill.com/regulation/court-battles/334529-supreme-court-strikes-down-nc-districts-as-illegally-based-on-race

White, Rev. Mel, a pamphlet "What the Bible says and doesn't say about Homosexuality".

Endnotes

[1] Jeff Flake, *Conscience of a Conservative: A Rejection of Destructive Politics and a Return to Principle*, p. x.

[2] *The American Spirit: Who we Are and what we stand for.* P. 102.

[3] Richard Rohr, *Daily Meditation*, "The Task within the Task", June 12, 2016.

[4] http://merceronvalue.com/archives/2005/04/abundance_vs_sc_1.html

[5] George Lakoff, *The ALL NEW Don't Think of an Elephant!*

[6] Ibid.

[7] https://www.cnn.com/2017/08/15/politics/donald-trump-david-duke-charlottesville/index.html

[8] Ibram X. Kendi, *Stamped From the Beginning*, p. 6.

[99] Glenn Gilbert, "Inflated MEAP scores full of hot air", *The Oakland Press* Published: Saturday, January 22, 2011
http://www.theoaklandpress.com/articles/2011/01/22/opinion/doc4d379eaa9b1a6148477516.txt
"State raises bar on MEAP, wants same for accreditation", *Detroit Free Press*, February 9, 2011
http://www.educationreport.org/pubs/mer/article.aspx?id=14546

[10] James Hohmann, "THE BIG IDEA: Donald Trump celebrated Sunday that his campaign to delegitimize the free press is working"

[11] American exceptionalism is the idea that the United States and the American people hold a special place in the world, by offering opportunity and hope for humanity, derived from its unique balance of public and private interests governed by constitutional ideals that are focused on personal and economic freedom.
http://www.wordiq.com/definition/American_exceptionalism
Also see: http://en.wikipedia.org/wiki/American_exceptionalism

[12] Palin, Sarah, America by Heart: Reflections on Family, Faith, and Flag, HarperCollins books, 2010.
Commentary on Palin's book: Darrell Delamaide' Dec 1, 2010
Political Capital Market Watdc hhttp://www.marketwatch.com/story/how-palin-dominates-the-political-narrative-2010-12-01"She is in every respect the anti-Obama: he is black, she is white; he is male, she is female; he is cerebral, she is emotional. She doesn't want change, because America is already great. So she doesn't need hope. She is the America we don't have to wait for; just recognize."

[13] Richard Lowry & Ramesh Ponnuru, "An Exceptional Debate, *National Review* Online (no date):
http://nrd.nationalreview.com/article/?q=M2FhMTg4Njk0NTQwMmFlMmY zZDg2YzgyYjdmYjhhMzU
Aaron Gardner, *Permanence, Change, and American Exceptionalism* March 29, 2010
Commentary on above quote inside this article:
The late Seymour Martin Lipset defined it as liberty, equality (of opportunity and respect), individualism, populism, and laissez-faire economics. The creed combines with other aspects of the American character — especially our religiousness and our willingness to defend ourselves by force — to form the core of American exceptionalism.
http://www.redstate.com/aarongardner/2010/03/29/permanence-change-and-american-exceptionalism/
Karlyn Bowman, Understanding American Exceptionalism
http://www.american.com/archive/2008/april-04-08/understanding-american-exceptionalism
Review of a book of essays published by American Enterprise Institute
Nick Baumann, "Obama and American Exceptionalism", *Mother Jones,* March 2, 2010 http://motherjones.com/mojo/2010/02/obama-and-american-exceptionalism
Quote:
This sentence tripped me up:
[America] is freer, more individualistic, more democratic, and more open and dynamic than any other nation on earth.
But the statement that America is "freer" or "more democratic" than literally every other society on earth, is argued largely through the quotations of founding fathers and Lincoln, as if saying something made it so.
Greene goes on to explain how even Freedom House, a US-based organization widely seen as center-right, ranks America far below first in terms of freedom and democracy. In fact, the US finishes in a multi-way tie for 30th.

[14] Ron Chernow, *Grant*.

[15] Thomas R. Eddlem. Meet the Author of U.S. Constitution's Preamble Learn about 18th-century statesman patriot Gouverneur Morris.

[16] from a speech at the Conservative Political Action Conference (CPAC) on 2/18/10. *Think Progress* Feb 19, 2010. http://pr.thinkprogress.org/2010/02/pr20100219.

¹⁷ Ann Gerhart and Philip Rucker, "The Tea Party is still taking shape", *Washington Post*, February 6, 2010. http://www.washingtonpost.com/wp-dyn/content/article/2010/02/05/AR2010020501694.html?wpisrc=nl_headline

¹⁸ Leonard Pitts: Some are crazy, incoherent to an extreme Thursday, March 4, 2010. http://www.journal-news.com/opinion/columnists/leonard-pitts-some-are-crazy-incoherent-to-an-extreme-580090.html

¹⁹ http://en.wikipedia.org/wiki/Dred_Scott_v._Sandford

²⁰
http://en.wikipedia.org/wiki/Citizens_United_v._Federal_Election_Commission#Majority_opinion

²¹ http://www.thenewamerican.com/culture/faith-and-morals/item/17055-supreme-court-will-consider-hobby-lobby-contraception-mandate-case

²² http://www.law.cornell.edu/supct/cert/preview_2013-14

²³ http://dailycaller.com/2013/10/14/mccutcheon-v-fec-why-it-matters/

²⁴http://www.legislature.mi.gov/%28S%28kzbjswln3cxrg3yvpn5w2sns%29%29/mileg.aspx?page=GetObject&objectname=2013-SB-0661..

²⁵ Lydia Wheeler, "Supreme Court strikes down NC districts as illegally based on race".

²⁶ Anne Blythe, "A judge, a Vegas phone call and the NC GOP legislative effort to remake the judicial branch".

²⁷ Ibid.

²⁸ Barton Gellman and Arshad Mohammed, "NSA call database explained".

²⁹ Elia Powers, "Wrangling Over Unit Records".

³⁰ James Hohmann, "THE BIG IDEA: Donald Trump celebrated Sunday that his campaign to delegitimize the free press is working."

³¹ Ibid.

³² Ibid.

³³http://www.jfklibrary.org/Historical+Resources/Archives/Reference+Desk/Speeches/JFK/JFK+Pre-Pres/Address+of+Senator+John+F.+Kennedy+to+the+Greater+Houston+Ministerial+Association.htm

³⁴ "'Road map is a life saver for us', PM Abbas tells Hamas", haaretzdaily.com, June 24, 2003).

³⁵ "Romney's Religions Speech". December 6, 2007. http://www.observer.com/2007/romneys-religion-speech

³⁶ http://www.mikehuckabee.com/?FuseAction=Issues.Home January 14, 2008

[37] "Huckabee: U.S. Gave Up on Religion". *Arkansas Democrat Gazette On-line*. Monday June 4, 1998.
http://www2.arkansasonline.com/news/1998/jun/08/huckabee-us-gave-religion/

[38] "Huckabee's mix of faith, politics similar to Bush". *Detroit Free Press* January 6, 2008.
http://www.freep.com/apps/pbcs.dll/article?AID=/20080106/NEWS07/801060591

[39] "TIME Poll: Majority Opposes Mosque, Many Distrust Muslims".

[40] Parvez Ahmed, "What Would Our Founding Fathers Say About the 'Ground Zero Mosque'?"

[41] "TIME Poll: Majority Opposes Mosque, Many Distrust Muslims".

[42] Jon Cohen and Kyle Dropp, "Most Americans object to planned Islamic center near Ground Zero, poll finds".

[43] "Muslim Americans Under Attack As Far Right Fights To Deny Them From Building Their Own Places Of Worship".

[44] Steve Krakauer, Gingrich Compares Ground Zero Mosque To 'Nazi Sign Next To Holocaust Museum'.

[45] Jane Mayer, "Covert Operations: The billionaire brothers who are waging a war against Obama".

[46] American Family Association, Press Release, April 16, 2015.

[47] Zack Ford, "The True Intent Of Indiana's 'Religious Freedom' Bill,

[48] United States Census Bureau,
https://www.census.gov/hhes/www/poverty/data/incpovhlth/2014/highlights.html.

[49] Arbinger Institute, *The Anatomy of Peace: Resolving the Heart of Conflict*.

[50] Leonard Pitts Jr. "Public silence greets poor's powerlessness".

[51] For speech go to http://www.huffingtonpost.com/2008/03/18/obama-race-speech-read-t_n_92077.html.

[52] Thandeka , *The Cost of Whiteness*.

[53] Leonard Pitts, Beck's exploitation of struggle is obscene, August 27, 2010.

[54] Ibram Kendi, op. cit. p. 10.

[55] Ibid. p. 261.

[56] "Obergefell v. Hodges", *Wikipedia*.

[57] John Boswell.

[58] John Boswell, Christianity, Social Tolerance, and Homosexuality.

[59] Rev. Mel White "What the Bible says and doesn't say about Homosexuality"

[60] Boswell.

[61] Michael Kinsley, "Kidding Ourselves About Immigration"

[62] David Weigel, "Alabama tried a Donald Trump-style immigration law. It failed in a big way."

[63] Jay Dickey and Mark Rosenberg, "How to protect gun rights while reducing the toll of gun violence", Washington Post, December 25, 2015. https://www.washingtonpost.com/opinions/time-for-collaboration-on-gun-research/2015/12/25/f989cd1a-a819-11e5-bff5-905b92f5f94b_story.html

[64] "Gun related deaths keep Going Up", http://time.com/5011599/gun-deaths-rate-america-cdc-data",

[65] "Gun violence in the United States".

[66] "Gun Violence".

[67] Christopher Ingraham, "27 Americans were shot and killed on Christmas day",

[68] "How bad is US gun violence?".

[69] Miguel Bustillo, "Shooting ok".

[70] Christopher Ingraham, op. cit.

[71] Erik Ortiz, "Walmart Shooting in Thornton, Colorado: Suspect Scott Ostrem Is Arrested".

[72] "Police Shootings".

[73] Teddy Cahill, et al., "Calls for calm after grand jury declines to indict officers in death of Tamir Rice".

[74] Mark Guarino, "Why a dash-cam video of a police shooting might not be a smoking gun".

[75] Mark Guarino

[76] Wesley Lowery, "DOJ will investigate July death of Darrius Stewart, an unarmed, black 19-year-old shot by police in Memphis".

[77] Mark Guarino, op. cit.

[78] http://www.cnn.com/2016/06/13/health/mass-shootings-in-america-in-charts-and-graphs-trnd/index.html

[79] "Mass shooting".

[80] Karma Allen et al., "Las Vegas shooting death toll rises to 59, no apparent connection to international terror".

[81] "Americans for Responsible Solutions", accessed February 22, 2016.

[82] Nancy Kaffer, "How to work on gun violence without violating the Second Amendment".

[83] Hillary Rodham Clinton, *What Happened,* page 189.

[84] Dan Stockman, "Dick's Sporting Goods' gun policy change followed sister talks".

[85] "Mass Incarceration – the whole pie 2017".

[86] "United States incarceration rate".

[87] "United States incarceration rate".

[88] "Incarceration in the United States".

[89] "United States incarceration rate".

[90] "United States incarceration rate".

[91] "The Fair Sentencing Act".

[92] "United States incarceration rate".

[93] "United States incarceration rate".

[94] "United States incarceration rate".

[95] "Incarceration in the United States".

[96] "United States incarceration rate".

[97] "Republicans Push for Sentencing Reform ".

[98] Neil Schoenherr, "Cost of incarceration in the U.S. more than $1 trillion"

[99] "United States incarceration rate".

[100] "Incarceration in the United States".

[101] "United States incarceration rate".

[102] "Crime in 2017: A Preliminary Analysis".

[103] "United States incarceration rate".

[104] "United States incarceration rate".

[105] Brennan Center for Justice for all.

[106] "New Agenda Outlines Ways Congress, Administration Can Act on Criminal Justice Reform".

[107] http://www.ratical.org/corporations/SCvSPR1886.html

[108] http://en.wikipedia.org/wiki/Citizens_United_v._Federal_Election_Commission#Majority_opinion

[109] Footnote in quoted document, [84] ROMANO GUARDINI, Das Ende der Neuzeit, 9th ed., Würzburg, 1965, 87 (English: The End of the Modern World, Wilmington, 1998, 82).

[110] Pope Francis, *Laudato Si*, #105.

[111] "Right-Wing Florida News Anchor Asks If Obama Is A Marxist; Defends Questions As 'Probing" http://thinkprogress.org/2008/10/25/biden-marx-mccain/'

[112] Billy Wharton, "Obama's No Socialist. I Should Know", *The Washington Post*, Sunday, March 12, 2009. http://www.washingtonpost.com/wp-dyn/content/article/2009/03/13/AR2009031301899.html

[113] Neil Weinberg, Michael Maiello and David K. Randall, "Paying for Failure", *Forbes*, May 19, 2008. http://www.forbes.com/forbes/2008/0519/114.html?boxes=custom

[114] Howard Zinn in *A People's History of the United States*.

[115] "The Glass-Steagall Act Explained"
http://www.nerdwallet.com/blog/banking/glass-steagall-act-explained/

[116] "Madoff whistle-blower attacks SEC".

[117] "There really isn't a crisis in health care in this country ... In fact, the odds of you being wiped out by a catastrophe or accident once the government gets started running this stuff is greater than if the private sector does -- but day-today, there's no health-care crisis in this country." --The Rush Limbaugh Show, June 18, 2009.

[118] David Cay Johnston, *Free Lunch: How the Wealthiest Americans Enrich Themselves at Government Expense (and Stick You with the Bill)*,

[119] ibid.

[120] David Cay Johnston, op. cit.

[121] *ibid*.

[122] "Lobbying Spening Data Base– Pharmaceuticals Health Products 2017.

[123] "Drug ads: $5.2 billion annually -- and rising".

[124] Pope Francis, *Laudato Si*, #138.

[125] Pope Francis, *Laudato Si*, #113.

[126] Pope Francis, *Laudato Si*, #156.

[127] Pope Francis, *Laudato Si*, #161.

[128] Bill McKibben, "Exxon's climate lie: 'No corporation has ever done anything this big or bad' October 14, 2015. "
http://www.theguardian.com/environment/2015/oct/14/exxons-climate-lie-change-global-warming

[129] "ExxonMobil's commitment to climate science", October 15, 2015
http://www.exxonmobilperspectives.com/2015/10/15/exxonmobils-commitment-to-climate-science/?gclid=Cj0KEQiAkIWzBRDK1ayo-Yjt38wBEiQAi7NnP9lKAV_vG1qy7Adl1xHWPU522s7UB0ItZPrkpMHzVaAaAtLW8P8HAQ&gclsrc=aw.ds

[130] Pope Francis, *Laudato Si (The Care of Our Common Home)*, May 2015. Norbert Bufka has written a study guide for *The Care of Our Common Home*. Go to Home page for more information.

[131] Joshua J. McElwee, "Francis: World close to suicide over climate change, *NCROnline*, Nov. 30, 2015.
http://ncronline.org/news/vatican/francis-world-close-suicide-over-climate-change

[132] "Infrastructure",

[133] George Lakoff, *The All New Don't Think of an Elephant!*

[134] *Brainy Quote*, Daniel Patrick Moynihan "Everyone is entitled to his own opinion, but not his own facts.",
http://www.brainyquote.com/quotes/quotes/d/danielpatr182347.html

[135] *Dictionary.com*. http://dictionary.reference.com/browse/opinion

[136] "TIME Poll: Majority Opposes Mosque, Many Distrust Muslims".

[137] Oliver Wendell Holmes. *Quote Investigator*.

[138] Michael J. Graetz, *The U.S. Income Tax*.

[139] David Cay Johnston, *Perfectly Legal*.

[140] Oliver Wendell Holmes. *Quote Investigator*.

[141] "Is There Really A Crisis?

[142] Barbara Arrigo, "Defending Social Security system begins with history lesson".

[143] "Status of the Social Security and Medicare Programs".

[144] "Current U.S. Federal Government Tax Revenue".

[145] "The 35% Corporate Tax Myth.

[146] "Bush Proposal Differs Greatly from Model".

[147] Joe Klein, "Social Security: How Would the Bush Plan Work?".

[148] *Think Progress*, May 4, 2010.

[149] Greg Kaza and Dr. Gary L. Wolfram "Property Tax Abatements".

[150] Shlaes, Amity. "When Chrysler's Jeep Runs Over the Little Guy."

[151] Eric Levitz, "Progressives Need a New Foreign Policy Vision. This Democratic Senator Says He Has One."

[152] *Detroit Free Press*, 7/17/05: see also "Dying to Win", *Wikipedia*, Robert A. Pape.

[153] Chris Hedges, War is a Force that Gives Us Meaning.

[154] Eric Levitz, "Progressives Need a New Foreign Policy Vision. This Democratic Senator Says He Has One."

[155] Eric Levitz, "Progressives Need a New Foreign Policy Vision. This Democratic Senator Says He Has One."

[156] Brennan Center for Justice

[157] ibid.

[158] ibid.

[159] *Avalon Project*, http://avalon.law.yale.edu/18th_century/fed68.asp

[160] Eric Black, "Why the Constitution's Framers didn't want us to directly elect the president", October 17, 2012.
https://www.minnpost.com/eric-black-ink/2012/10/why-constitution-s-framers-didn-t-want-us-directly-elect-president

[161] George F. Will, The electoral college is an excellent system, The Washington Post, December 16, 2016.
https://www.washingtonpost.com/opinions/the-electoral-college-is-an-

excellent-system/2016/12/16/30480790-c2ef-11e6-9a51-cd56ea1c2bb7_story.html?utm_term=.aef0a41374b6&wpisrc=nl_opinionsA&wpmm=1

[162] Michael D. Schaffer, "Often a target, the Electoral College endures. How did we get here?", December 18, 2016. http://www.philly.com/philly/opinion/commentary/20161218_Often_a_target_the_Electoral_College_endures__How_did_we_get_here_.html

[163] Eric Black, op. cit.

[164] Michael D. Schaffer, "Often a target, the Electoral College endures. How did we get here?", December 18, 2016. http://www.philly.com/philly/opinion/commentary/20161218_Often_a_target_the_Electoral_College_endures__How_did_we_get_here_.html

[165] Michael D. Schaffer, op. cit.

[166] "One man, one vote", Wikipedia, https://en.wikipedia.org/wiki/One_man,_one_vote

[167] "Population vs. Electoral Votes", *Fair Vote*, http://www.fairvote.org/population_vs_electoral_votes

[168] Robert Samuels "In last-shot bid, thousands urge electoral college to block Trump at Monday vote, How the electoral college works", December 17, 2016. https://www.washingtonpost.com/politics/in-last-shot-bid-thousands-urge-electoral-college-to-block-trump-at-monday-vote/2016/12/17/125fa84a-c327-11e6-8422-eac61c0ef74d_story.html?utm_term=.019d9e924664&wpisrc=nl_headlines&wpmm=1

[169] "National Popular Vote movement" Fair Vote http://www.fairvote.org/national_popular_vote#endorsers_of_the_npv_plan

[170] http://www.nationalpopularvote.com/president-elect-trump-reaffirms-his-long-standing-opposition-electoral-college-and-favors-nationwide http://thehill.com/blogs/twitter-room/other-news/266423-trump-calls-for-revolution-blasts-electoral-college http://www.nationalpopularvote.com/newt-gingrich-endorses-national-popular-vote http://www.nationalpopularvote.com/president-elect-trump-reaffirms-his-long-standing-opposition-electoral-college-and-favors-nationwide

[171] Michael Shearer, "Seven things that could go wrong on election day".

[172] Jessica Schulberg, "Good News for Russia, 15 states use easily hackable voting machines".

[173] Ibid.

[174] Steven Rosenfeld, "A Voting Machine Meltdown in 2016 Is Likely, Investigation Warns".

[175] [122]SECOND VATICAN ECUMENICAL COUNCIL, Pastoral Constitution on the Church in the Modern World Gaudium et Spes, 26.

[176] Pope Francis, *Laudato Si,*.#156.

[177] Chris Cox, "No, Mr. President, the NRA is not to blame: Chris Cox", *USA Today*, December 3, 2015. http://www.usatoday.com/story/opinion/2015/12/03/no-mr-president-nra-not-blame-san-bernardino-column/76748608/

Chris Cox is the executive director of the *National Rifle Association's Institute for Legislative Action*.